•*LEARNING FROM CHILDREN*•

Michael Onguto

LEARNING FROM ♥♥ CHILDREN

by
Paul
Welter

Tyndale House
Publishers, Inc.
Wheaton, Illinois

ACKNOWLEDGMENTS

Approximately six hundred adults took time to tell me or write down storeis about what they had learned from children. I have changed some children's names to ensure anonymity. Kearney State College made available reassigned time for my study in this area. Mrs. Anita Norman provided reference assistance. Readers of major portions of this manuscript include Dr. Jack Balswick, Ms. Linda Isham, Dr. Vic Cottrell, and Dr. Leonard Skov. *Faith At Work* gave permission for use of selected excerpts. Sue Frerichs, Lillian Robertson, and Marilyn Davis were the typists.

Kent Estes has been my partner in this venture. Each week we met at the Corral Cafe in Kearney to talk over the class, "Learning from Children," and to plan the session for the next week. It was during these weekly conversations with Kent that my thinking was most advanced. I know I learned some of the concepts here from Kent, e.g., the idea that children are constantly challenging their deepest fears.

I learned from each of my four children as they went through childhood. Lillian, my wife, made a number of suggestions that contributed to the unity of the book. Sue Frerichs, our youngest daughter, gave important help as a member of the Learning from Children class. She is a careful observer of human behavior, and the mother of two small children.

Bill, our youngest son, worked with me during the course of the writing to provide the cartoons and drawings of animals found among these pages. He has a number of childlike traits, including a light touch and a finely tuned sense of humor. I continually learned from Bill how to enjoy life as we collaborated on this venture.

First printing, August 1984
Library of Congress Catalog Card Number 84-50537
ISBN 0-8423-2141-1, paper

• C O N T E N T S •

The first book in this helping series, *How to Help a Friend,* proposed a method for helping others based on a relational foundation. Among the themes of the book was that of the rhythm of giving and receiving. *How to Help a Friend* was mostly about giving. The focus of this second book in the series is on receiving. Receiving from others provides the renewal we need to continue the helping process. In addition, we can learn a great deal about helping and caring skills from children. Therefore, *Learning from Children* is meant to stimulate a renewal by presenting children as model helpers, helping us learn to receive from children, and teaching us how to have fun.

THE
RENEWING PROCESS

THE DEEPENING QUEST

*T*t was a warm summer day, and I was sitting on the steps of the front porch, tired after returning from a long trip. David, my grandson, who was two years old at the time, was playing in the front yard. My wife, Lillian, set up the hose and sprinkler to water the lawn. David ran through a bit of the area where the water was spraying and called excitedly, "Grandpa, take off your shoes!"

I said, "No, thanks, David, I'll just sit and watch." A bit later, Lillian began to run with him through the water. David called again to me. Finally, I took off my shoes and socks, rolled up my trouser legs, and slowly trudged out. David took our hands, and the three of us went running through the water. I felt the joy coming. We started to leap and yell as we ran. I began to feel younger. Two neighbor children were watching us, looking for an invitation. I signaled to them to come on over, and then there were five of us leaping and playing—a regular chorus line!

Ashley Montagu, anthropologist and commentator on human nature, wrote about playfulness in his book, *Growing Young:*

Perhaps the best insight into the nature of play is that provided by Plato in The Laws, *the book of his old age. The model of true playfulness Plato saw in the need of all young creatures to* leap.[1]

I don't think I understood what Plato and Montagu were talking about until now, in my mid-fifties, when a child had taught me to leap again, and I felt the pure *joy* that accompanied the leaping. I began to feel sad for the physically impaired children of the world who *can't* leap. Then I felt sad for all those adults of the world (including me) who *could* leap, but *don't!*

Another realization that came to me on that summer day was an awareness that a quest of mine, undertaken earlier, was gaining momentum. That quest originated with my discovery of a radical, puzzling declaration by Jesus. Ever since I had become a Christian at age nineteen, the statement in Matthew 18:3 had interested, intrigued, and nagged me: "Unless you change and become like children, you will never enter the Kingdom of heaven" (TEV).

A year and a half ago I had spoken to a State Association for Early Childhood Educators on the topic, "Learning from Children." We decided on a theme for the convention of "Tots Are Teachers, Too." As I gathered information for the address, and as I met with this delightful group, I found myself suddenly thrust into a new adventure. It was no longer enough to wonder what Jesus meant; it was now necessary to begin the process of becoming like a child and helping others join this venture. But although the imperative from Jesus was given a long time ago, the course seemed quite uncharted.

My initial thinking was that, to become like a child, I would need to observe children more closely and learn from them. It seemed useful, also, to find what things other adults had learned from children. So I started learning *intentionally* from my two grandchildren. Next, I became a helper in a church school class for four-year-olds.

Then I began a two-year process of collecting stories concerning what adults had learned from children and how they had learned it. I led a number of workshops on "Learning from Children," and the participants seemed eager to respond to my request that they write a story for me about what they had learned from children. About this time I worked with Bruce MacDougall, the president of Faith At Work, leading a Faith At Work conference. He is a "released" person who has childlike qualities. His book, *Rejoice in the Lord*,[2] has a chapter in it entitled "Hurrah for Kids." The book, and the author, helped free me to become more childlike.

I shared my quest with Kent Estes, a close friend who has been in a support group with me for five years. He suggested I teach a college class on "Learning from Children." My excitement grew. I reread Montagu's book, and noted his purpose: "And now we begin to see that the goal of life is to die young—as late as possible."[3] Montagu's goal spoke to me of joy and playfulness.

In the class which Kent and I team-taught, wonderful things began to happen. Forty-two people invested three hours one evening a week for an entire semester to share in the quest to learn from children. They were childlike adults of all ages—and they shared amazing stories of what they had learned from children. One of the class members introduced me to Dennis Benson and Stan Stewart's book, *The Ministry of the Child*.[4] The authors used the name "Starchildren" to indicate that children come to us fresh from God's presence.

The class members' childlike qualities had an impact on all of us. One person wrote the following note:

I've been around cynical and unhappy people for so many years now that the experience of being around caring and giving people, including class members and you, Paul, and you, Kent, has caused the painful reopening of the flower of hope and trust and love that has been lying dormant in my heart. I'm also feeling that thick shells do cover deep hurts, and I reach out to people more, particularly those same cynical and unhappy ones.

Kent and I began to identify, observe, and interview adults who were especially childlike (Montagu calls them "neotenous"). These were people who had been on this journey a long time. Many were without a *conscious* quest to become like a child. But nearly all had the realization, sometimes an uneasy one, that they were spontaneous people who were sometimes viewed as "different" by others.

The study and writings of Robert Coles became more and more appealing to me. I was already familiar with his *Children of Crisis*,[5] a multivolume work written during the 1960s and 1970s. This Harvard University child psychiatrist has spent twenty years interviewing children— poor children, migrant children, rich children. His Pulitzer Prize-winning volumes tell what he has learned about the strengths of children. A magazine article which he wrote, "The Faith of Children," focuses specifically on the spiritual qualities of children:

And I think that children who are 5 and 6 and 7 who have been brought up in the Christian tradition are able to ask the same kinds of difficult questions that Christ himself asked as he surveyed the Palestinian scene a couple of thousand years ago. They are moral questions: How am I going to live my life, what do I believe in, how is this all going to end up, and what is the meaning of life really?[6]

■ CHILDREN—OUR SPIRITUAL MENTORS

Children do have a great deal to teach us by their questions, their answers, and their lives. How may we utilize them as resource people in our spiritual growth? That is the question this book seeks to answer. As a preparation for getting the maximum amount of personal growth from the pages that follow, you may find it useful to respond to the specific questions below:

Do You View Children as Master Teachers?

Adult after adult expressed to us surprise at the experience of learning from a child. And these adults who told us their stories probably spend more time with children and are more knowledgeable about them than the average adult.

The first step toward viewing children as master teachers is to get down to their eye level, or even a bit further down so that you can look up to them. The next step is to do something *with* them. As you do this, observe them closely and listen carefully to them. Finally, reflect on what you are learning about life from them.

Do You Have Access to a Child or Children?

You are fortunate if children are a part of your daily life space, because you thereby have regular access to their teaching. Of course, even good things can be overdone. Yesterday I began to think I had too much access to little children! I spent my regular hour assisting with the pre-kindergarten Sunday school class (I play my guitar and lead the singing, clean up glue, and in other ways try to be useful to the teacher and children). Then my wife and I had nursery duty during the church service. Following that, our grandchildren were with us from noon until 11:00 P.M. I was bushed! Yet I learned a great deal.

At the end of a long day of reading aloud, Lillian said hoarsely, "My voice is so tired I don't think I can read anymore." David, now nearly three, and still awake at 11:00 P.M., shared the tired feeling. He replied, "My voice is so tired, that all I can say is, 'I love you!' " The quest to live out Matthew 18:3 begins and ends with love and joy.

If You Do Not Have Access to Children, How Can You Gain Access? Appendix I, Ideas for Further Action and Study, includes some specific suggestions for gaining regular access to children. Are you taking seriously Christ's command?

How Will You Take Seriously the Words of Jesus That We Are to Become Like Little Children if You Do Not Spend Time with a Child?
Jesus did not merely mention a child to the disciples. He brought one into their circle. This indicates that the *presence* of children is important if we are to learn from them. This book should be useful in helping build a greater readiness for this learning process. It can prepare you for the learning that will have the greatest impact in your becoming childlike—the time you spend with children themselves.

STORIES—A WAY TO LEARN WITHOUT TRYING

*T*his book contains many stories about what adults have learned from children. We have found that storytelling is a valid teaching-learning method. So we believe that you will learn from these stories—whether you read for learning or enjoyment, or both. Intentionality needs to be present if we are to learn well when material is presented in a logical, sequential, analytical way. But with a story we may be surprised into learning. And we may learn something far different than what another person has learned from the same story. In fact, there are no general conclusions given here concerning *the* path which everyone should take in the journey into child-likeness. The path through life is always unique for each person, and everyone finds his or her own way. The stories and connecting ideas are meant to illumine different paths for different readers.

■ THE POWER OF STORIES
Sister Jose Hobday has lectured widely on "The Spiritual Power of Storytelling." She emphasizes the importance of sharing stories, and of sharing "our story."

Unless somehow we develop the spiritual power to keep fingering those words of each other's story. . .unless we do that, then we won't find this vitality and fun and enthusiasm and playfulness and creativity in our spiritual life.[1]

I came by my own desire to tell stories naturally. My father was a great storyteller. In fact, some years after he and my mother retired from the farm at age seventy (he lived to be almost ninety), I suggested he compile his stories. Several years later he presented me with five Big Chief tablets containing his story—really a collection of scores of stories. After my work of editing, my wife's artwork and typing, and our children's work collating the purple-inked, duplicated pages, we presented him with 100 copies of a homemade 100-page book. He gave these out to his family (including grandchildren), relatives, friends, and neighbors—until they were gone. He had told his story—a powerful one. That book is filled with all kinds of stories—some matter-of-fact, some comical, and some sad. Here is one of the funny ones:

THE MOUSE IN THE CAR, *by Edward Welter*

During the course of one's lifetime, we have the opportunity to see many very comical incidents. I can still recall a few. One summer day not too long after cars became common, my wife Elsie, my daughter Margaret, and I were driving to town (nine miles away). We were about halfway there when Elsie jumped and screamed, "There's a mouse in the car!" I never was fully convinced which hit the top of the car first—her head or her heels. Although the little mouse could not squeal loudly enough to be heard in all that commotion, yet he was bending every effort to save his own hide. As his well-being depended on his quick getaway, he dashed up my pants leg and for the moment, at least, he was safe.

Well, it seemed to me that what was needed was for someone to remain composed. Although I could feel the slimy little stinker gradually making his way up my body [Dad wore unbelted bib overalls] and could hear the completely uncontrolled confusion continuing in the car, I kept right on guiding the car up the road. About that time, the confused little creature crawled out the neck of my shirt, and in the twinkling of an eye, spied the open car window, made one desperate jump, and succeeded in getting out of the car at last. Can't you hear the heartbeats?

There is much to learn from this story. I noted, for example, that at times my father was able to take the point of view of the mouse—a mark of an effective storyteller. I learned, too, that there is a certain justice in life. Just when my father was chuckling about my mother's predicament, the mouse headed in *his* direction.

At any rate, I wanted to tell you why storytelling is important to me. I hope you enjoy reading stories about what adults have learned from children, and that you learn from those stories. You may also be interested in *how* the adults learned from children.

■ HOW ADULTS LEARN FROM CHILDREN

As you read the stories that follow, you will note some clues that indicate how the adult learned. Here are some "hows" we have noted:

The child creates a peak emotional moment which expands the peripheral vision of the adult, making it possible to view the world in a deeper, wider, richer way.

The adult is shocked or surprised by the child into considering a new truth.

The child serves as a model, or example, for adults to follow in some specific area, such as honesty, spontaneity, or the expression of love.

The child entices an adult into playing, and the adult

finds joy and begins to learn a new way of life.

An adult feels loved by a child and gains the insight that he or she is cared for and is worthwhile.

■ AROUSAL

We discovered when we sat in a group telling stories that an arousal mechanism was triggered. A story told by one person would awaken a story within another. In this way, stories would surface in the group that individuals could not have recalled if they had been by themselves.

This mechanism will work to your advantage as you read. The stories you will read concerning what others have learned from children will arouse within you similar learning experiences. Therefore, the learning that may transform your life will come not only from what you read here, but also from:

1. Your own awakened stories.
2. Other ricochets in your mind.
3. Recognizing when you are near a child that you are in the presence of a master teacher.
4. Discovering new ways for a giant (yourself) to enter a child's world.
5. Receiving from a child.
6. Experiencing the resulting renewal in your life.

The stories highlight the positive characteristics of children. I am well aware that children have negative characteristics; but there are enough books which treat children as problems without adding another one to that growing list. Also, Jesus was obviously talking about positive characteristics when he said we were to become as little children.

■ BORN FREE

Young children model those traits which Jesus said are necessary to enter the kingdom of heaven. They are born free of those cultural restrictions and personal biases which are pressed upon us quite early in life. We are taught, for example, to compare ourselves with others, to be less than honest, and to be negative. In fact, we soon become "adult-er-ated." When do children begin to lose their childlikeness? I think some begin to lose it in their second year of life. Others keep many of their childlike qualities on into older childhood and adolescence. And some never let these traits go. I know three persons in their nineties who are childlike—spontaneous, laughing, friendly, optimistic, loving, courageous, and creative! The potential for living out that kind of story is there for each of us.

THE CHILDREN AROUND US— WHO TEACH US FAITH

· T H R E E ·

BECOMING HUMBLE—
THE BELIEF THAT
YOU ARE INCOMPARABLE

You really *are* incomparable! Perhaps not according to Webster's first definition of the word, "eminent beyond comparison," but certainly according to the second definition, "not suitable for comparison." I was excited to read in Dag Hammarskjöld's book, *Markings*, his view that, "To be humble is *not to make comparisons*."[1] That definition of humility seemed right and freeing to me.

Comparing ourselves with others is a way of life for many of us. We enter a restaurant, church, grocery store, or classroom and begin stacking this new world of people vertically, with ourselves uncomfortably squeezed somewhere in the stack. This person is better-looking than I, that one thinner, another more intelligent, and still another "more spiritual." There may be some whom I would estimate below me in some category, and as *they* begin to sense the judgment, I begin to feel arrogant or condescending.

But something deep inside most of us whispers that people are unlike cars, typewriters, or blenders—people are not for comparing. We are created by God, with each creation being one of a kind. We have heard people say, "When God made that person, he threw away the mold." That's true. And it's true of every one of us. We are as unique as our fingerprints.

If we learn how to group our world of people horizontally, we can enter a new kind of life. What will that new life feel and look like? We will feel less pressured because no one will be above or below us. We will see others as whole persons. (If we look at people who are above us we see waistlines and nostrils. If we look at people beneath us we see bald spots and shoulder tops.) We will find ourselves freer to move when we do not have to climb under or over others.

George Groddeck, a German analyst and a contemporary of Freud, wrote an essay in which he discussed the derivation of words that have to do with "child," or "childlike." He noted the similarities in two important words, and he attested to the humility of children—and some adults:

The relationship of Kind, *child, and* König, *king, has been mentioned. History, as well as everyday experience, teaches us clearly enough that the essence of kingship is childlikeness. The more a king relies solely on his presence, the less he talks, the greater is the effect he produces and the greater he himself becomes. It was only after Frederick the Great had given up speaking and philosophizing, and was content to be silent, hoping nothing, desiring nothing, realizing his own childlike nature, that he became our truly great "Alter Fritz."* [2]

Reading this essay by Groddeck helped me better understand the humility of a child—or an adult. The humble person does not try to impress. He relies only on his presence.

■ FREE NOT TO HAVE TO MEASURE UP

As a child growing up on a Kansas farm, I liked it when my father periodically measured my height. He would place a yardstick horizontally on top of my head and mark the place on an old cupboard. Then he used the yardstick to measure the distance from the floor to the mark. I remember I would always stand as tall as I could—stretching my backbone! I wanted to catch up with my older brother. But that stretching made it harder just to be me, because the next time I was measured I would have to stretch again—more if I could—to show growth from the last time. I never relaxed while being measured.

Actually, it was kind of fun to be measured once in a while. But I recently thought about how tense it would make me to stand in that position for hours, days, years, or a lifetime. And then I realized that is exactly what I had been doing for many of my fifty-four years! This insight came to me in the Faith At Work conference mentioned earlier. Bruce MacDougall was saying that the gospel is not something we have to keep measuring ourselves against all the time. It is the place of grace. That truth took hold of me that day, and I experienced a renewal, and a new sense of freedom.

Little children live in this kind of freedom. And something inside us wants to get that freedom back. Lawrence LeShan writes about this urge in his book, *How to Meditate.* At a conference of scientists, all of whom practiced meditation daily, LeShan asked why they meditated. Many answers were given, none satisfactory until,

Finally one man said, "It's like coming home." There was silence after this, and one by one all nodded their heads in agreement.[3]

LeShan discussed that process of returning to something we once had:

We meditate to find, to recover, to come back to something of ourselves we once dimly and unknowingly had and have lost without knowing what it was or where or when we lost it. . . .

It is this loss, whose recovery we search for, that led the psychologist Max Wertheimer to define an adult as "a deteriorated child."[4]

The freedom of children is most apparent in their ability to be spontaneous and fun loving. One adult told this story:

Jim, eleven years old, was doing some homework in the kitchen. His parents were necking on the couch while watching TV. Jim walked by on his way to his room, observed the scene, and casually said, "Go for it, Dad!"

Although children are free and spontaneous, these qualities do not necessarily last. When they get a bit older, they begin to compare themselves, as I did, to an older brother or sister, or a friend. Then the process begins which is outlined so well in Adlerian psychology: comparison and competition, with competition being the struggle for social power and individual significance. It is based on the idea that:

I matter—I count—because I'm more important to a significant adult (usually a parent) in my life than a third person is to that significant adult. Or, usually later, I'm more important to my friend than a third person is to that friend.

■ JESUS AND THE LITTLE CHILD

At this point we are back to the setting in which Jesus called the attention of his disciples to a little child (Matthew 18:1-5; Mark 9:33-37; and Luke 9:46-48). Each of these synoptic Gospel accounts indicates that the disciples were involved in comparison and competition, and were struggling for personal significance. They were arguing, according to Mark and Luke, about who among them was the greatest. Matthew noted a broader aspect of the argument: "Who is the greatest in the kingdom of heaven?"

It was at this precise point that Jesus gathered the twelve disciples, took the child in his arms, and made his radical statement about the qualification for entering the kingdom of heaven. Jesus called for humility and pointed to the child as an example of this trait. Young children are humble in that they are not comparing and competing. They take their significance for granted and face their world in an open, relational way. Children are free of pride, which is based on comparison and competition. ("I'm glad I'm not like that tax collector over there." Translation: "God, I don't have to remind you— do I?—that I'm a better person than he is!")

■ BECOMING LIKE A LITTLE CHILD

Jesus asked the impossible, or the extremely difficult, of nearly everyone he met:

To a paralyzed man: *"Get up, pick up your bed, and go home!"* (Matthew 9:6).

To a tax collector, sitting in his office: *"Follow me"* (Matthew 9:9).

To the twelve: *"Heal the sick, bring the dead back to life, heal those who suffer from dreaded skin diseases, and drive out demons"* (Matthew 10:8).

Also to the twelve (who were probably quaking in their sandals as they were about to leave on their preaching-healing mission): *"So do not be afraid of people"* (Matthew 10:26).

To the disciples, faced with a hungry crowd: *"You yourselves give them something to eat!"* (Matthew 14:16).

To Peter (across a stretch of water): *"Come!"* (Matthew 14:29).

To Peter (concerning forgiveness): *"No, not seven times . . .but seventy times seven. . ."* (Matthew 18:22).

To the very rich young man: *". . .go and sell all you have and give the money to the poor, and you will have riches in heaven; then come and follow me"* (Matthew 19:21).

To a dead man: *"Lazarus, come out!"* (John 11:43). And many more.[5]

Each of the above persons obeyed his particular difficult or impossible command with the exception of one—the rich young man.

Now—if Jesus made a practice of asking his followers (or would-be followers) to do the extremely difficult or impossible, it seems reasonable that his command to become like a little child will not be easy to implement (although on the surface it does seem a bit easier than being born again).

What is involved in the process of becoming like a little child?

1. Relying on the power of the Holy Spirit.

2. Resisting the temptation to compare ourselves with others.

3. Opening ourselves relationally to the people around us, even though the new vulnerability is frightening. Children are extremely vulnerable. (One of the theses of Bruno Bettelheim's *The Uses of Enchantment* is that children live in a world of giants—adults—so giant stories and other fairy tales have great meaning to them.)[6]

4. Being with little children and learning from their presence. Jesus modeled this by affirming the presence of children.

The above suggestions are only incomplete guidelines. Each story you read will serve as a turn of the kaleidoscope to give you a fresh view of some of the infinite variety of patterns of humility and other qualities that may be seen in a child's life.

A college student spoke wistfully of the vulnerability of her little sister:

My sister is seven years old. Recently, she asked me to walk around the block with her to sell Girl Scout cookies to the neighbors. It amazed me that she knew every family on the block, and I didn't even know our next door neighbors. Children have no inhibitions about walking up and talking to people, whereas adults are always afraid of what people will think, and so they go through life never knowing the people down the block. If they do, it's often because their kids play together. If only adults could be as open and friendly as children!

These open and friendly qualities come, in part, from the humility of the child. Humility also enables a child to accept others without criticizing them. A teacher trainee was nurtured by this kind of acceptance:

At my first field experience—observing in a classroom—I saw a young boy who knew just what to say and what to do to make a person feel good. I was there only one hour when he came up to me and hugged me and told me, "I love you."

Children don't judge you. They just like you the way you are. It's adults that teach them how to be critical of people.

The basis for judging and criticizing is pride—the urge to compare, compete, and be "better than." Learning humility from children can free us to be comfortable with our incomparable selves.

REGAINING TRUST—
PURE AND SIMPLE

*W*hat is trust? A child helped define trust for his father:

We had been looking for nearly an hour and we were frantic. Knowing one's four-year-old child is lost in the mountains is terribly frightening. It was only our second visit to the cabin since it had been completed so we weren't very familiar with the surroundings, and neither was our boy. Our dream of a getaway spot had turned into a nightmare. And then, as suddenly as he had disappeared, we found him. After the excitement had calmed down, I said to him, "I was scared to death; weren't you afraid?" He responded, "I wasn't very afraid because I knew you were looking for me."

Trust—"assured reliance on the character, ability, strength, or truth of someone or something" *(Webster's New Collegiate Dictionary).* Trust is at the center of faith, and no one has more of it than a child.

The fear of abandonment is the strongest of all our fears, but children can live with the fear. Until the child learns differently through a bad experience, he knows (in a way that he could not explain) that his parents have made an implicit promise and a covenant to be with him, and to search for him if he is lost. It is this kind of simple trust that God asks of us; and the basis for our trust is also a promise—this time an explicit one. God has made a covenant with his people to be with them. There are promises specifically made to enable us to turn from fear to trust:

Do not be terrified; do not be discouraged, for the Lord your God will be with you wherever you go (Joshua 1:9, NIV).
. . .God has said, "Never will I leave you; never will I forsake you." So we say with confidence, "The Lord is my helper; I will not be afraid. What can man do to me?" (Hebrews 13:5b, 6, NIV).

Jesus' parable of the lost sheep provides comfort for those of us who may be "lost" at a given time. It also provides an immense amount of comfort to those who are not lost. We are able to risk and love and venture, knowing that our God is one who will never call off the search for us if we are lost.

Adults in our study reported experiences with children who were models of trust and faith. One reported what it was like to have children trust her:

I have learned from children how trusting they are. They accept what you tell them—your promises, your supposed knowledge that you try to pass on to them. They don't wonder if it is true, they just accept it. They are also quick to forgive and forget if a promise is broken.

And many children have to cope with broken promises. A ten-year-old boy told about such an experience:

Mom and Dad had a fight and were yelling at each other. Dad said he was going for a walk, then slammed the door and left. He was gone a long time, so Mom and I got in the car and went to look for him. Mom was crying and so was I. We looked all over but couldn't find him, so we finally went back home. Dad was sitting on the front steps. Mom went in the house and I sat down by Dad. He said, "Don't cry. I won't ever leave you." But two months later he moved out.

I kept hoping Dad would come back, but after two weeks, my Mom told me that Dad had left to live with another woman. Then I understood, but I was mad at him for awhile.

Two adults gained faith in the resurrection from children:

I thought I had faith, but my four-year-old niece increased mine. When her Dad died suddenly, we were at the funeral home and her mom lifted her up to see the body. She stuck a stick of gum in her daddy's pocket and said, "I'll be seeing you."

This fall the brother of one of my students was killed by a train. When she came to school the very next day, I wanted to pick her up and cry with her. But she said simply, "Teacher, my brother was killed last night, but he's in heaven with God and he's very happy," and then went to paint. Maybe she doesn't fully understand that her brother is gone forever, but her child's view of death and faith really made me think and review my feelings on death and faith.

■ THE BEATITUDES

There is something about the people that Jesus called "blessed" that reminds me of the trust and faith of children. See what you think.

Blessed are the poor in spirit,
*   for theirs is the kingdom of heaven.*
Blessed are those who mourn,
*   for they will be comforted.*
Blessed are the meek,

for they will inherit the earth.
Blessed are those who hunger and thirst for righteousness,
  for they will be filled.
Blessed are the merciful,
  for they will be shown mercy.
Blessed are the pure in heart,
  for they will see God.
Blessed are the peacemakers,
  for they will be called sons of God.
Blessed are those who are persecuted because of righteousness,
  for theirs is the kingdom of heaven.[1]

We can learn from children how to be blessed if we are teachable. They can show us how to grieve, how to be merciful, and how to be pure ("unadulterated"). And we can learn from them how to be persecuted because of righteousness. How many millions of children have been hit because they spoke the truth? A little child can lead us into the above blessings.

SAYING THE UNSAYABLE—
BECOMING HONEST AGAIN

s we collected stories about what adults learned from children, one of the qualities mentioned most was honesty. Sometimes remarks brought a chuckle:

From children I have learned that it is important to tell it like it is! I learned this by simply listening to them. As an example of a child telling it like it is, I am reminded of this incident. A little boy offered to do a small errand for his grandmother and told her: "I want to do it for you because you don't have many good years left!" He certainly told it as it appeared to him. (She was fifty-five at the time!)

■ TRANSLATING

Children must often find themselves translating adult statements when euphemisms are used, punches are pulled, facts are withheld, or truth is befogged in other ways. Given such misinformation, or lack of information, children have to rely on perceptiveness to make sense of their world. Sometimes they help each other out, as in the following incident related by a fourth-grade teacher:

I don't know how to word what I learned, but I know I'll never forget this incident. The first day of school last week I was explaining the discipline plan I use and going over my class rules with my students. Rule #6 is, "Keep your hands and feet to yourself." After I read this rule, one boy asked, "What does that mean?" Before I could answer, another boy spoke up, "It's just a polite way of saying, 'Don't fight.' " I agreed and as I turned around I heard the first boy ask his neighbor, "Why didn't she just say that?" The second boy responded with the voice of experience, "I've learned from experience that grown-ups rarely say what they really mean!" I wanted to rush and scribble out rule #6 and write instead— "DON'T FIGHT."

What makes this one of my favorite stories is the adult statement, "Keep your hands and feet to yourselves." This has to be mystifying to children, inasmuch as these appendages are fastened onto the body and are unlikely to depart! Also the philosopher-style conclusion about adult speech is thought provoking.

The adult use of sarcasm also requires children to work at translation:

I learned from my son that I shouldn't use sarcasm with children. Two weeks ago on Saturday, he had to do his chores before going outside. He had spent much time watching cartoons and when his friends came over, he still had his work to do. He did a halfway job of cleaning the living room and continually got angry when I told him what else needed to be done. Finally I got fed up with him. Sarcastically I told him he really did a fine job in helping me clean. I was angry with him and told him he had to stay outside until I was finished painting the baby's room and cleaning the house.

Last Saturday my son did a great job of cleaning the living room. When he was upstairs changing his clothes, I told him what a good job he had done. He came to the top of the stairs and asked me if I was saying it out of "madness." I asked him what he meant. He wanted to know if I was saying it because I was mad or if I really meant it. That really opened my eyes to sarcasm.

Sarcasm is anger expressed sideways. The child accurately perceived the real emotion—"madness."

■ HONESTY IN COMMUNICATING FEELINGS

Children are straightforward in expressing emotions, whether those emotions are negative or positive. The following story illustrates how a child expressed her negative emotion. (I personally would have preferred sarcasm! But the teacher was wise, unshockable, and patient, and like all good teachers, used a crisis as a learning instrument for *both* teacher and child.)

During my first year of teaching, I learned a lot. I learned in particular to respect pupils' work even if it was not correct. Their work is an extension of themselves and should be respected even if the teacher does not consider it of high quality. The following episode shows how I learned this the difficult way:

I had only two first-graders, as I taught in a rural school. Other pupils were in grades two, three, and four. The first-graders had learned to print answers on the blackboard. One little girl had printed her answer on the board but it was wrong. I immediately erased it. Suddenly—POW—the little girl clenched her fist and socked me in the stomach. I had just destroyed something that she was proud of! She was humiliated! I learned after that to let students erase their own work and print the correct answer themselves.

Needless to say, I had to think up some form of punishment because she had hit me. Instead of spanking her, as her sisters expected me to do, I kept her in all day—no A.M. recess. No noon recess. No P.M. recess. That was a long day for a small girl. Maybe this was not severe enough, but she and I both learned a lesson.

Sometimes children want to communicate negative emotions to adults but have to invent novel ways of communicating so the adult will listen, as in this creative confrontation between a boy and his dad:

Father came home from work tired and wanted to do nothing but relax in his easy chair and read the paper. His five-year-old son asked him to play with him and the father replied, "No, I just want to read the paper now and do nothing else. I will play later."

Five minutes later his son presented him with a plain white tissue. The father asked, "What is this for?" The son replied, "Let's pretend this is a newspaper." The father said, "OK, what does the newspaper say?" His son replied, "Sometimes I like you and sometimes I don't."

Powerful! The child knew his father was not attending to him, but he also noted what the father was attending to, and created a way to communicate using the adult's preferred mode (visual) and specific medium (newspaper). I talked to that dad about the incident, and he said his son secured his full attention with that method.

It is, of course, not enough to be honest. We have to find a way to convey the *message* so the true *meaning* is received by the receiver. How did the five-year-old know this? Is all of his childlike wisdom deep inside all of us? How do we make it operational?

Confronting—such a difficult task—is often done well by children. Children seem to know that *eye contact* should be a part of confrontation:

One afternoon at home I found my schedule full of countless tedious tasks. The dishes, dusting, washing, etc., stared me in the face. In my usual frenzy, I began tackling the tasks while my four-year-old daughter kept after me. "Mom, let's bake cookies." I'd reply, "Later, honey." "Later, sweetie," I'd say as I shoved the vacuum. Finally in exasperation she looked me in the eye and said with conviction, "Mommy, later is right now!" It hit me like a bombshell. I should not put off until tomorrow the joys I can have right now.

Children do work at confronting adults, and they also work at challenging adult generalizations, when necessary:

I learned just yesterday from a six-year-old student of mine not to categorize people. This little boy was frequently using bad language in class and on the playground. I told him that nice people do not say bad words. His reply was, "My dad is nice." I didn't know how to respond to that.

Fortunately, children are as honest in communicating tender feelings as they are in confronting and in communicating negative emotions.

Children share feelings in such an honest way. Our seven-year-old began kindergarten with no trouble, but in first grade she cried every morning for the first week. Last week she approached me with, "I have made a decision not to cry when I start second grade this year. Some kids aren't with their moms very much, but I'm with you all day and we do everything together. So I get lonesome when I'm gone from you all day. What would really help me out tomorrow [first day of second grade] is if you would come and have lunch with me so I could see you in the middle of the day."

Preschool, kindergarten, and first-grade teachers are aware that children are often worried about the loneliness of the *parent*. Children may disguise this as their own loneliness in a gentle effort to protect the adult's strength. This could be an untold part of the story above. Children are able to capture a moment by expressing honestly the emotions and thoughts that are stimulated.

My neighbor told the story of a very important time she spent with her son when he was five years old. They were attending her husband's grandpa's funeral. The boy was sitting between his mother and father. When the soloist finished singing, he looked up at his mother with big tears in his eyes and said, "Mommy, wasn't that absolutely *beautiful!" She said he really seemed to sense the importance of that service and they were so glad they had decided to bring him with them because it was a special moment for both him and his parents.*

Finally, children provide us with honest reminders, even though the reminder may be self-serving. A seventy-year-old still remembered clearly a time when his small son misbehaved and deserved a reprimand. His son said—with perfect timing—"Dad, it's times like this when you should remember the *good* things a little boy does!"

THE CHILDREN
AROUND US—
WHO TEACH US HOPE

RECOVERING OPTIMISM

*M*edical researchers are continuously looking for useful drugs that have minimal side-effects, and this effort has been directed especially toward a search for chemical tranquilizers and mood-elevators. Unfortunately, these nearly always have side-effects, some of which may be serious.

Now that there is a growing emphasis on health, the search for mood-elevators will likely turn to nonchemical substances. Can you visualize the following prescription scrawled on a small piece of paper?

R: Spend fifteen minutes daily with a child. (May be refilled as needed.)

I've given such "prescriptions" to adults who have lost hope. Words from a counselor are not enough when hope is gone. The "hopeless" person needs to be in the presence of a "hopeful" person. Children are hopeful. And they have the additional advantage of producing no harmful chemical side-effects (although this point may be argued by some adults)!

Montagu has pointed out both the reality and the function of optimism in children:

Most children carry with them the feeling that whatever the state of things "now," they can only improve with time. The child lives in a world of rising expectations, and because he does so he puts the self-fulfilling prophecy—when permitted—to constant good use. When he is optimistic about the outcome of anything he is likely to do the necessary to make it come true.[1]

One mother was a bit embarrassed by the optimism of her daughter:

I once dated a fellow who had lost his arm as a child. My young daughter was very interested in making him feel OK about it. One night as they sat on the couch she was examining his arm closely. She found a small bump and assured him that he was probably growing fingers. I feel this is being about as optimistic as you can get! My first reaction was one of embarrassment, but she was completely sincere.

Another small child "looked up," and brought optimism and confidence to her mother:

Our youngest child is three and a half. Three days a week, she must get up at 7:00 A.M., dress, eat breakfast, find her coat, mittens, and hat, gather a doll or "take along"—amid four other people in the household doing their own thing. As we walked out the door following one of those busy mornings, she stopped on the step, looked up at the sky, and said, "It's a pretty day, Mom." My day began "pretty" and I know I was a neater person to be around because—it was a "pretty" day!

We found that some persons had enrolled in our Learning from Children class because they believed they had become too negative, and they were looking for a way to become more positive. One mother was in that category. In fact, she looked on her own childhood as causing her pessimism.

A main reason for my taking this class is that I felt blocked or stifled as a child. My childhood experience has a direct bearing on what I want for my kids. I am a perfectionist, always trying to be organized—painstakingly; and I never quite make it, resulting in frustration. I tend to point out my mistakes. I have a need to analyze and criticize. I want my kids to be able to maintain a sense of wonder, appreciation, and creativity—to be able to create for themselves and enjoy it. I want to learn how to develop and keep a good rapport with my children now, before they become teenagers, and to listen. I want to learn how and what my kids are thinking, so we can grow together. I believe it is important to develop self-esteem, and some area of interest that they can excel in. I'm trying not to be pushy, but to set a good example.

There is a wistfulness about the above paragraph, She had been "cheated" of optimism in her childhood. The title of the course, "Learning from Children," provided some hope that she could recover this optimism and that she could release it in her own children. She demonstrated a high level of awareness and a deep sense of mission for effective parenting.

Bettelheim has discussed the importance of hope:

When one such child after prolonged therapy finally emerged from her total autistic withdrawal and reflected on what characterizes good parents, she said: "They hope for you." The implication was that her parents had been bad parents because they had failed both to feel hope for her and to give her hope for herself and her future life in this world.[2]

It should be said here that there are, of course, many other causes of autism than the one implied here. But the point that Dr. Bettelheim makes says a great deal about the value of optimism and hope and the provision of that kind of a nourishing environment for children.

When the atmosphere in a home is positive and hopeful, it matches the child's own optimism—that which Montagu has called "a world of rising expectations." This "match" of a child's inner and outer world helps the child avoid confusion and find wholeness.

Let's suppose we had an optimistic, hope-filled childhood. How do we retain or release this optimism? One person in our class told about a childlike friend of hers who has such qualities as playfulness, creativity, joyfulness, optimism, and a dancing spirit. The class member said this of her: "She remembers being told to grow up, but she didn't pay any attention!" I like that.

FINDING COURAGE BY
CHALLENGING OUR FEARS

George MacDonald's point of view is ". . .the child is not meant to die but to be forever fresh born."[1] This implies that sometimes our childlike qualities do die. If so, who or what is the executioner? I think the evidences are very strong that it is *fear* that annihilates these traits, or at least forces them to retreat and go into (sometimes lifelong) hiding.

We may feel like:

> dancing in the aisles at church
> singing in a crowd
> crying
> following a dream
> beginning oil painting at age thirty or sixty-two
> becoming a teller of stories at nineteen, or forty-
>   five, or seventy-four

What's keeping us from releasing these and scores of other actions and traits? Probably fear of others, or perhaps habits that began a long time ago with a need to be safe.

At one time I worked as a school psychologist doing individual testing and diagnosis of children who were seen as having "learning or behavior problems." Once when I was administering an individual intelligence test to a first-grade boy, I asked him, "What does 'brave' mean?" He replied, "It's when you're scared to death but you do it anyway." I learned something about courage from that child that day. Courage means we challenge our fears toe-to-toe. Children, who live in a world of giants, rely on their courage every day.

Children apparently are born with a number of fears, including the fear of being dropped, the fear of loud sounds, and the fear of abandonment. Note little children's challenging response to the fear of being dropped—they stand up before they are "ready"; they try to walk when their sense of balance is edgy; and they defy gravity by climbing all available obstacles.

Little children also challenge their fear of loud sounds. They *produce* loud sounds and they also expect others to do this. Robert D. Strom has written a useful book with an intriguing title, *Growing Together: Parent and Child Development.* He notes regarding sounds:

It is common for parents who witness excited children simulating sounds for trucks and trains to caution "not so loud." The noise of children's play that reflects the intensity of involvement is sometimes considered an indicator of hearing loss. A more reasonable assessment is that the young train conductors are doing what is required in adult life, and therefore in role playing: shouting above competing engine noises. If a mother were aware of this, she would know how foolish it is to announce in a whisper, "All aboard." One mother playing with her child credited herself with blowing up a bridge without making a lot of noise. Much to her dismay, the young play partner continued to cross the bridge—refusing to acknowledge its demolition, since he hadn't heard the dynamite charge.[2]

Now, concerning that deepest, most permanent and pervasive fear—the fear of abandonment. Infants and very young children also challenge this fear. The challenge begins in the first few months of life with the game, "Peek-a-boo." It continues when the child achieves mobility, usually walking or beginning attempts at running, with hide-and-seek.

Thus the child lives on the edge, constantly challenging his greatest fears. And in George MacDonald's words, perhaps that is how the child, and the child within us, keeps from dying and is "forever fresh born."

■ THE WAY OF DISCOVERY

This quote on an anniversary card from my wife has had a life-changing impact on me:

> *We cannot OWN each other;*
> *We cannot CHANGE each other;*
> *We can only DISCOVER each other.*

A life of discovery means a lifetime of challenging our fears. As one adult said about her future:

I want to discover and release the creativity within myself—discover my four-year-old self that is free and uninhibited and able to jump for joy, and be spontaneous. I am too serious about life, too responsible, too logical, and too methodical. I also want to develop the right side of my brain and become more creative and more intuitive.

Where do children find the courage to challenge their fears and thus live a life of discovery? They are fresh creations from the love of God, and that lets them be brave:

There is no fear in love; perfect love drives out all fear. So then, love has not been made perfect in anyone who is afraid, because fear has to do with punishment (1 John 4:18, TEV).

Children can teach us about love, and thereby, about courage. The relationship, the presence of someone we love, lets us challenge our fears:

Five-year-old Scott and his uncle were working on the roof. Scott's mother later said that he had never been on a ladder or a roof before, and that he was scared of heights. The uncle had to come down for more tools, and he forgot his nephew for fifteen minutes or so. When he scurried back up onto the roof, he found Scott crying. The uncle asked Scott if he was afraid. He responded, "No, but I got lonesome."

Scott was able to challenge his fears when he was in the presence of a person he trusted. When that person was gone, he was no longer able to challenge those fears.

The book, *There Is a Rainbow Behind Every Dark Cloud*, is filled with drawings and thoughts by eleven children ill with cancer, leukemia, and other sicknesses, who helped each other face death. The book resulted from group meetings in which they gained courage through love. The adult group leaders expressed what *they* learned:

We have found that love is the fuel that allows for the joining of minds, and that age is not a factor in telling us who our teachers are.[3]

Children have usually been denied the role of teacher because of their age. Isn't it time now to reject such age discrimination and to open ourselves to learn from teachers of all ages?

THE CHILDREN AROUND US—WHO TEACH US LOVE

RELATIONSHIPS ARE MORE IMPORTANT THAN TASKS

*T*he greatest commandments ("Love the Lord. . .and your neighbor. . .") have to do with relationships rather than tasks. Tasks are terribly important. Yet, in the crisis times of life, as well as the quiet, peaceful times, we straighten out our priorities and realize that relationships are more important. Children know this. A parent writes:

I found myself out of work this year and home all day with our five-year-old. One of the best times is when he wakes up in the morning and crawls on my lap. We sit and rock and cuddle and just belong to each other. Very seldom are words said for a long time. We enjoy just being in each other's presence.

■ THE URGENT AND THE IMPORTANT

Charles E. Hummel has written a booklet called *Tyranny of the Urgent*. He quotes a person who said, "Your greatest danger is letting the urgent things crowd out the important."[1] Hummel noted that the three-year ministry of our Lord seemed all too short:

A prostitute at Simon's banquet had found forgiveness and a new life, but many others still walked the street without forgiveness and a new life. For every ten withered muscles that had flexed into health, a hundred remained impotent. Yet on that last night, with many useful tasks undone and urgent needs unmet, the Lord had peace; He knew He had finished God's work.[2]

Perhaps there is a way of learning from children how to differentiate what is urgent from what is important. Little children view *relationships* as most important, despite the urgency that adults around them ascribe to *tasks*. I believe that one reason Jesus said we are to become like little children is that they have their priorities straight in this regard: relationships first, and tasks second.

■ MAKING TASKS SERVE RELATIONSHIPS

The fact remains, however, that tasks must be done, so how do we take care of both? The trick is, when possible, to put them together so that the task serves to deepen the relationship.

Sue, my daughter, captured the "tasks can deepen relationships" idea:

I've learned that the child psychology and education books and teachers were all wrong about young children's attention spans. I was always taught that young children have a very short attention span. But when I read or play with our little boys, I find that their interest in what we are doing usually lasts much *longer than mine. Reading the same book several times in a row is boring to me. I wonder—maybe the reason they can stay interested in one thing so long is because they see what we're doing as* time spent with me rather than just accomplishing a task *such as finishing a book or game. They probably know that I tend to end my time with them at the end of a book or game, so they want to make it last as long as possible.*

Yea for David and Daniel! And for Sue and her husband, Doug, who take time—and make time—for those relationships. What are some of the tasks that blend well with relationships? Here are some samples:

Reading

The example given above by Sue has to do with reading. Children and parents have known about this perfect match-up of task and relationship for hundreds of years. I remember reading C.S. Lewis's seven-volume *Chronicles of Narnia*[3] through three times as bedtime stories to our two youngest children during their growing-up days. There was some grief when I realized Sue and Bill were moving out of the realm of childhood, and we would not be reading it again together.

Family Traditions

Family rituals and traditions are not tasks in the true sense of the word, but they involve a time set aside for an experience, and they do help provide structure, security, and warmth in a family. They also serve as a time for celebration. A new family ritual can be added at any time. My wife, Lillian, and I decided to do just that several years ago. We love our son-in-law, Doug. So we decided to celebrate that love with a "Son-in-law Appreciation Evening" held in our home each year about the time spring turns to summer. We share a meal together. After the meal we give Doug some gifts. Then we tell Doug something about him—a quality or trait or something he has done—that we thank the Lord for. It is a great evening and ends with hugs all around. It's a tradition we plan to continue.

If you can't think of a new tradition to begin, I recommend you read *Building Happy Memories and Family Traditions.*[4] You will find exciting possibilities discussed there.

Hospitalization

Two creative mothers tell their stories about how a trip to the hospital for a tonsillectomy served to deepen an important relationship:

The first time my oldest daughter was in the hospital was an important time for me. She was apprehensive about the hospital and the surgery but thrilled to be with me without her sister and brother. We took special care in buying her gown and robe. We went out to a favorite place to eat and then I was allowed to spend the night with her before surgery. We had a regular old slumber party for two. We played games, talked, and read books together. My daughter and I became friends that night as well as mother and daughter.

Isn't that a great sentence—"My daughter and I became friends that night. . ."? A second mother tells about a similar experience:

One special time was preparing my six-year-old daughter to have her tonsils out two years ago. Since I had never gone through surgery with a child, I experienced a lot of trauma myself. This helped make me sensitive to her feelings because we were both going through it for the first time.

I found our book Curious George Goes to the Hospital *and we read and discussed it. Rather than new pajamas or other clothing, I bought her a Curious George stuffed animal. He was a surprise. I explained that he would be with her all the time. She clung to him the whole time. The experience went well and is positive in her memory and mine.*

Baking Cookies
Every mother and a few dads know about this one. The woman and child in the following story experienced fun and a deepening of their relationship:

One day this past summer, our hired man's two-year-old girl came home with me. She was adjusting to new surroundings and a new baby sister, which meant she was no longer the center of attention. I was planning to make cookies and she was eager to help. I showed her how to roll the dough in her hands to make a ball, and then as I put it on a cookie sheet, I carefully patted it down a bit. She watched the whole procedure carefully, and then proceeded to take a piece of dough and pat it out to look something like the finished product. She let me know she didn't see any reason for making it into a ball first. When we finished she had cookies and milk so she could sample her work. As she went home, she took a sack full of cookies to her brother and sister. It was fun for me because it had been twenty-three years since my girl was two, and it was important for her because she got some extra love and attention that day.

The above are just a few ideas for putting tasks into the service of relationships. To these could be added:

    cleaning a garage
    changing a diaper
    shopping for groceries (although taking more than one child is not recommended for deepening relationships!)
    raking the yard
    bathing a dog, and many more

Actually, the important thing is the presence of an attitude that life is primarily relational.

EXPRESSING LOVE

*T*his chapter and the next (on caring) are similar. Here is the difference as I am using the terms. By expressing love, I mean *communicating affection* by saying, "I love you," or by the use of other words, or by touch. By caring, I mean a compassionate reaching out to meet another's need. Children have a great deal to teach us in both these areas.

As we sorted the children's stories according to what the adult learned (sometimes this was stated explicitly and sometimes implicitly), we found one of the largest categories was, "I learned from a child (or children) how to express love." Apparently children are at their best in teaching and modeling this skill. There is a special beauty in these stories that tell about expressing love. It is as if the children released something very deep, very ancient, and very young within the adult:

My nephew and I were busily walking around the house looking for Magic Markers. He stopped me, took my hand, and said, "Wait a minute. I want to tell you something." I said, "OK." So I sat down as he stood in front of me. He looked at me with his big blue eyes and said, "I love you so much. I want to show you how much I love you." I could just feel this little heart aching—ready to burst with the love he wanted to give.

We talked about it for awhile, and we hugged and cried together. Later I thought about what he had said to me. A busy eight-year-old boy, taking time out to tell me that he loved me and that he wanted to show me that love. How often do I think of showing my love to others? I thanked the Lord for the lesson and I'm still thanking him for it!

■ NOT EXPRESSING LOVE—A SIN OF OMISSION?

A Bible verse I worry about is James 4:17: "So then, the person who does not do the good he knows he should do is guilty of sin" (TEV). This verse, of course, teaches that we can be sinners by doing nothing. I am a sinful man, O Lord! Can children help us avoid such sin? Here is a child who can be a model for us:

My nephew Bill ran up to his cousin Erin (whom he doesn't see very often) and hugged and kissed her on the cheek saying, "I missed you, Erin!" He taught me that as adults we sometimes don't say what we are feeling.

The important lesson here is not that adults say something other than what they are feeling, but rather that they may omit entirely expressing real feelings of affection. Is such an omission a sin? Think of the the number of persons who are leading shackled, fearful lives (afraid of being abandoned) because the significant persons around them fail to communicate their love. Little children often take the initiative in expressing love:

When I came to school feeling unhappy about my life after an argument at home, a little girl came up to me and said, "You look nice, I love you." That taught me how much we need to give and receive love and appreciation.

The other children in the classroom may not have realized it, but they were in debt to that girl. She had brought her teacher back into the human race—into the realization that she was loved. And that teacher was probably able to be more effective and kind that day because a child had not omitted doing an important thing.

■ THE RELEASING EFFECT OF EXPRESSING LOVE

When a child expresses affection to us, a need is met and we may learn to express our love to others. In addition, something else often happens. We are released and "opened." A woman thoughtfully recounted how a little child opened and transformed her father before her eyes:

Through a child I learned that the way I saw my father was not the way everyone saw him. I have never considered my father to be a very emotional, loving person. Recently, for the first time, I had occasion to watch him play with a two-year-old. He was so loving and open. He had "human" qualities that I had never seen in him before. Since then I feel differently about him. I wonder if maybe I envy that little girl because she was so open and loving with him and he responded so beautifully.

The unfulfilled longing in the adult daughter is a powerful part of this story. Another aspect is her amazement at the revelation of the endearing qualities in her father which she had never seen before. It was as if the two-year-old had pulled the curtains and a "new" father had walked out on the stage, a father who had been wearing a mask all the twenty-five years of his adult daughter's life.

Other things happened. The storyteller felt emotionally closer to her father. Also, there are clues in her last sentence that she now feels some responsibility for the fact that a distance exists. This could be the first step to her becoming more open and loving with her father.

It was a big gift from a small child—the gift of reconciliation—or at least the creation of a setting where reconciliation becomes possible.

■ THE PARADOX INVOLVED IN BECOMING SPONTANEOUS IN EXPRESSING LOVE

One of the very attractive aspects of a little child's expression of love is that it just happens:

I learned spontaneous affection from children. I have two little girls in my kindergarten class this year who are extremely affectionate. They always hug and kiss me when they leave. Then a few others will follow suit. At first I didn't know if I should encourage, discourage, or ignore this. Then I decided just to let it be spontaneous. I'm a touching person anyway. So if they want to hug and kiss, and others do too—I'm there for them.

How can we *plan* to be spontaneous? One way through this paradox is to work at letting it happen, rather than making it happen. Instead of trying to be spontaneous (which would be like attempting to sketch a square circle), I need to be myself, to feel my emotional pulse, and to release the warmth from inside me.

The above teacher did this. She ". . . decided just to let it be spontaneous." Also, she was willing to receive love: "I'm there for them." I've noticed that one of the marks of an effective elementary teacher is the ability to receive love as well as to give it. This allows the child to be whole and to be happy—it is, after all, more blessed to give than to receive.

A useful book for those wanting to learn to express love more effectively is *I Want to Say I Love You* by Jack Balswick.[1] He explains how quickly children become inexpressive adults unless they have parents who model expressiveness for them. So the lines of influence go *both* directions—from children to adults, and from adults to children!

· T E N ·

CARING

Caring is used here to mean something very similar to the following idea of Montagu's:

In brief, then, compassionate intelligence is involvement in the other's plight combined with the desire to help in some practical way.[1]

Intelligence is an important component of caring because it gives one the ability to choose or create the most effective response from among many options. There are many examples among our stories of children who modeled and taught effective care-giving. One such child sensed his mother's fear of computers, and responded in a caring way:

My son received a computer, and I asked him to teach me how to use it. He used his softest, gentlest voice; he looked at me and touched me at the end of each point. He made me feel good about "me," whether or not I learned the computer.

I write on the chalkboard on the first day of each college class that I meet, the following sentence:

THE PEOPLE IN THIS ROOM ARE MORE IMPORTANT THAN THE COURSE OF STUDY.

Somewhere along the line I rediscovered this important truth. The child computer instructor had not yet lost that truth.

■ AN AWARENESS AND CONCERN
FOR THE PLIGHT OF OTHERS
Jesus' story about neighborliness ("The Good Samaritan" in Luke 10) reminds us that it is possible to walk right by others who are in trouble and choose not to get involved. Here is a story about a neighbor who cared enough to get involved:

I learned sincerity, spontaneity, and inquisitiveness from a child. My puppy had just had eye medication and was ill. I had carried her outside on the grass. The little girl across the street came over and asked what her name was, why her eyes were green, and how come she couldn't stand up. My response was that she was sick and had just been given medicine. This especially stands out to me because the girl was so sincere. I had just returned from the vet who had told me the pup had a 30 percent chance of living.

All children seem to share the concern of this girl for animals, especially small animals, younger children, infants, and in general, the helpless beings of the world. They understand what it is to be helpless and to be at the mercy of others. As we get older and more self-sufficient that empathy and altruism may decline.

The adult in the above story learned from the sincerity of the child. She knew her neighbor girl *really cared* about the puppy's welfare. And through their conversation the adult felt cared for.

This story is about classroom neighborliness:

One day my seven-year-old daughter, Marcy, came home from school with a book that she said her teacher had given her. She informed my wife and me that she had received it for helping and working with Jeff, a fellow second-grade student at her center table.

Marcy told us that Jeff is a boy who does not like to do what the teacher says and that sometimes "he even swears." But Marcy has been able to accept Jeff as a person and care enough about him to help him with his paper work and reading.

I don't know if Jeff is changing or not, but I learned that my daughter is a person who cares about others and she taught me about caring and accepting people as persons.

Marcy's father, who told this story, is a pastor. One could see that his respect for his daughter had grown even greater. He was touched deeply by her caring, and as he pointed out, it was a learning experience for him in the areas of acceptance and caring. Marcy didn't just have a "warm spot" in her heart for Jeff. She *did* something—she took the initiative to make life better for him. And this is what caring involves—action.

■ GIVING COMFORT

One important way to care is to show comfort. All adults are aware that children seek comfort—a "Band-Aid," a kiss on the hurt place, or a hug. We are usually not as aware that children just as readily *give* comfort. The child who comforts the injured adult in the following situation dispenses an unusual "medical" prescription.

A friend of mine was visiting her family. On one visit this summer this lady was playing a game with her niece and nephew—tag or hide-and-seek—and hurt her foot. Her niece came over to comfort her and told her, after looking at the foot, "It'll be OK. I think you should have a popsicle and go to bed. That will make you feel better."

Well, at least the remedy was inexpensive and the niece's *intention* must have been comforting.

■ COMMUNICATING A DEEP UNDERSTANDING

When we are deeply understood by another person, or when we deeply understand another, we have a peak experience. It is a special moment. Often our eyes will fill with tears. There is a healing—sometimes for both people—certainly for the one who feels understood.

The man who tells the following story had such a peak experience:

At thirty-five I haven't yet admitted that I'm too old to participate in the town basketball team. Last Sunday I came home with my left eye blackened and badly swollen. After I had explained what had happened, my seven-year-old daughter said, "Now that will teach you not to go play basketball!" After some short thought I replied, "I doubt it." She looked at me, took my hand, and knew exactly what I meant. Such glimpses of oneself are rare and very enlightening.

The first step in becoming a more effective listener is to be the benefactor of such listening. This adult was listened to, understood by, and comforted by his child, and in the communication of that understanding and comfort, he was changed. This will be an important step in his becoming better able to *give* comfort through listening and understanding.

■ THOUGHTFULNESS

When someone thinks of us and lets us know it, we usually feel cared for and worthwhile. The adult in the following story learned this concept from a child, then began practicing it herself.

Something I've learned from a child is to be interested in others and to want to know what is happening in others' lives. One holiday I was asking the children in my class what they would be doing. One of my students, six years old, said, "What are you *going to do?" I realize how thoughtful that child was of others. It really feels good to have others ask about you—to know someone cares and is interested. Since then I've realized how much more important to me are those people that ask about* me. *I've since tried to ask people about themselves.*

A similar experience happened to me one evening when my own son, Bill, was a child. I had stopped by his room after he had gone to bed. As I gave him a backrub, I asked him how his day had gone. After he had responded to my question, he asked me how my day had gone. I felt cared for by his thoughtfulness. It was an affirmation of me as a person.

So—there are many ways to learn caring from children. The first step is opening ourselves to experiencing their caring for us. Then we follow their example in our caregiving.

RENEWING FRIENDLINESS

*F*riendship is an affectionate attachment. Although it can't be separated from love, it has a special quality all its own. Friendship may spring from seed to full flower almost instantly; or it may grow slowly over the years from the acquaintance level through other levels—ally, associate, colleague, companion; and then through various levels of friendship—distant, good, close—to that of intimate friend.

■ CHILDREN TEACH US TO LET FRIENDSHIPS BLOSSOM RAPIDLY

Little children are open to becoming friends very rapidly. I once saw such a friendship emerge, blossom, and come to an end, all in less than a minute. The drama developed in an airport. I was walking along one of those endless passageways when I noticed two families walking opposite directions. One family (apparently) consisted of a mother and father, a two-year-old girl, and a five-year-old boy. The other family was made up of a grandmother and grandfather and a girl about a year and a half old. As the two little girls approached each other they looked at one another, stopped, and stood facing each other about two feet apart. I was at the side of the corridor, and I stopped to watch.

The two girls continued to look at each other. They smiled. Then the two-year-old stooped down and rubbed her hand over the younger girl's shoe. It was a shiny, patent-leather shoe and she liked the feel of it. Then she stood up, they looked at each other again, and they spontaneously hugged each other. One of the parents told the two-year-old that they needed to go. The families moved away from each other, with the girls giving an occasional backward glance until each had merged with the crowd.

It had been a peak experience for me, and I'm sure it was also for those actually involved in this brief, flourishing friendship. And it was a learning experience. What did I learn?

1. That the time lapse from "stranger" to "friend" does not have to be a long one.
2. That just because we're going to have to let go of a friend, it doesn't mean we should not get close.
3. That a friendship is a gift, not only to the friends themselves, but also to those who observe it.
4. That touch can be a cause and an effect of friendship.
5. And I relearned that when relationships are put ahead of tasks, even urgent ones, lives can be changed.

■ FRIENDSHIP IS RECIPROCAL

It isn't friendship if one person just gives and the other just takes. That can lead to an attitude of condescension on the part of the giver and sponging on the part of the receiver. Infants and little children, who may not look much like givers because they are so dependent, can nevertheless be full-fledged participants in a friendship.

My daughter, Sue, has had little children as friends all through her high school, college, and older adult days. She described a special time with one of her friends:

When I was in college I played volleyball, and one year I hurt my ankle. So I lay in bed with my ankle propped up and iced, feeling bad that I was missing out on volleyball, and everything else that was going on around campus. I couldn't do anything and I felt useless. My coach came to see me and she mentioned that she had to go somewhere for awhile and had to get a baby-sitter. I told her that I would watch four-month-old Kelly. She didn't want to leave her since I was hurt, but I told her I really wanted to do it, so she finally left Kelly with me. It was such a neat time, because even though my ankle was swollen to double its normal size, and I couldn't even walk, it didn't matter. . . .Kelly couldn't walk either. I lay on my back and Kelly lay on her tummy on my chest, and we just smiled at each other and had a good time. My roommate took a picture of us, and I used to keep that picture on my bulletin board to cheer me up. Kelly taught me that even when I was confined to bed I could still do some important things.

Sue and Kelly experienced the joy of being friends. And they built some good memories. Not bad for an afternoon!

■ CONFLICT—A WAY TO BECOME FRIENDS

Adults often hold grudges as they emerge from a conflict. Children are more likely to come out of a fight as friends. Note below that it was the child who, after a conflict, took the initiative to move toward friendship. The adult, fortunately, was able to receive and to respond to the initiative.

After having a severe discipline problem with an emotionally disturbed child at a camp, a beautiful thing happened the next day. Out of the blue, this little girl came up to me and said, "Anita, it's so much easier to be nice than mean all the time." That was one of the most memorable times I've had with a child. We gave each other a hug. That was six years ago. We just touched each other's lives. The girl was eleven and I was twenty years old.

The story below shows how it's possible for a child to deal effectively with a conflict. She worked hard at maintaining friendly relationships with both parents by attacking the problem. She could have "attacked" her parents, or have used some kind of "fight or flight" tactic instead of using her effective method of averting a potential conflict.

My fourth-grade students were doing an art activity and making cards for their parents. Kim came up and asked if she could make two cards since her parents were separated. I learned that she loved her parents equally and thought it out a great deal before coming to her conclusion. She even made the cards exactly alike, with just the same amount of "I Love Yous" written all over.

■ FRIENDSHIPS CAN DEVELOP IN THE EYE OF A STORM

Even though people live or work in settings where some are hostile to others, this negativity does not have to be contagious. Love and loyalty do not require that we choose sides and form two armed camps. Children can bring this truth home to us.

It was Christmas; one of my sisters and her sister-in-law do not get along at all. Their relationship has gone from bad to worse. This Christmas was just another time when we'd all have to put up with the strained relationship. They each have a three-year-old daughter. Those two little girls are best friends; they look out for each other. They played together all day with joy and happiness. As I watched them that day I wished that we as adults could have that accepting, loving attitude toward another person just because she is a person. They do not reflect the attitudes of their mothers. They seem bound not to miss out on the fun and friendship they can have because of two adults and their petty arguments. One wonders who is acting more "mature."

■ CHILDREN BELIEVE OTHERS WANT TO BE FRIENDLY

The lonely person is not only scared to be alone; he is often afraid to be with people. Sometimes part of that fear is the mistaken notion, "Others don't really want me as a friend." An adult gained some new insights from little children on this issue:

By observing the social behavior of my daughter and other children at the age of eighteen months to four years or so, I learned something startling. From twelve to eighteen months children seem to be very fond of and excited by all other children. They're curious about them, interested in them, and approach them openly and without hesitation. They are totally sociable and eager to interact with one another. I don't think it's extreme to say my daughter is a fanatic about other children! It seems to me that this tendency decreases with age as a result of parental teachings such as, "Leave them alone," and, "You don't need to bother other people," and so on. I wonder if people really have a basic need to be outgoing and friendly. If so, they not only lose it, but many people seem deliberately to close themselves to strangers. I believe that if everyone felt others really wanted to be friendly, we could learn from kids how to reach out.

This adult learned that little children are *friendly*. They want friends and they want to be friends. By being with children, perhaps we can understand that adults (deep down) have these same wants and needs. And children can teach us how to open ourselves again to others.

SHARING A SENSE OF WONDER

I grew up on a Kansas farm. Under a part of our old farmhouse there was a cellar. We entered it from outside the house through cellar doors and a cellar way (stair steps). The cellar doors sloped up slightly.

On summer evenings after we had done the chores and had a good meal, Dad and I would often lie down on those double cellar doors and watch the stars come out. We would begin counting them as they first appeared. (It just now occurred to me—was Dad using this to help me with my number concepts?) Then they would "pop out" faster and faster in the beautiful, sparkling night sky, and one of us would point and say, "There's one—over there!" Finally, they appeared so fast that we couldn't count them anymore, and we would just relax and enjoy the beauty of the starry sky, and wonder at our God who could create such a marvel.

Something happened during all those evenings, in addition to the counting and the appreciation of the wonder of God's creation. I couldn't have explained it then, but I felt it.

As Dad and I experienced together a sense of wonder at being enveloped by such beauty, the bond between us deepened. And as I held his hand many years later when he died (he was eighty-nine and I was forty-two), that deep bond still existed between us.

Two (or more) *people who share a sense of wonder are bonded together in a powerful way.*

Shared wonder is a relationship builder, just like shared joy, shared tragedy, or a shared adventure. The similarity is that each is a peak experience—a point at which all nerve endings are on the surface.

There is something about the stars that awaken wonder. Dennis Benson and Stan Stewart in the useful and "wonder-ful" book, *The Ministry of the Child,* use the term "Starchildren" to refer to those children and adults who possess childlike qualities:

Where do these "other" qualities come from? Certainly not entirely from us. Our children are also children of the universe. They come to us red-hot from the heart of God. For this reason, the authors name them Starchildren.[1]

A childlike friend of mine told about getting her family up in the middle of the night to view a comet shower.

Two summers ago there was a spectacular comet shower. It was supposed to occur about two o'clock in the morning. And so I got our blankets out and laid them on the lawn, and then I rounded the family up. They were saying, "Oh, Mother, do we have to get up?" and I said, "Yes, you really have to see this. I've never seen a comet shower. You, I want you to see one!"

And so we went out and lay on the blankets and watched. . . and watched because it didn't happen right away. But the stars were beautiful, and finally the comet shower started, and it was just fantastic. I think that will always be a memory for us—our family. It was a special time for us.

This parent gave her family several gifts that night—a special memory that will always be there, an enlargement of each family member's sense of wonder, and a new family closeness.

How does a child keep alive that sense of wonder? Rachel Carson speaks to that point in her book *The Sense of Wonder* (which is filled with photographs—gorgeous pictures of the ocean, awesome photos of the sky, and quiet pictures of little things, such as particles of sand under a lens). She says:

If a child is to keep alive his inborn sense of wonder. . .he needs the companionship of at least one adult who can share it, rediscovering with him the joy, excitement and mystery of the world we live in.[2]

And, I would add, if an adult is to keep alive his inborn sense of wonder, he needs the companionship of at least one *child* who can share it. The following story illustrates this truth.

My friend, an electronics engineer, had attended a Christian conference with his four-year-old son on his lap. The focus of the conference was on seeing God in all of creation and on the importance of taking time to enjoy God's creation. On the way to the car his four-year-old stood looking up at the stars. My friend yelled at him to get in the car. His son's response was, "God made the stars and I like to look at them."

Sharing a sense of wonder with a child need not always take a lot of time. One man wrote:

An important time I had with a child was the time my three-year-old granddaughter took my hand and said, "Let's go out and look at the world" (our backyard). After our look at the world she said, "I love you, Grandpa."

One time four people went up onto a mountain to pray. Two others appeared, and an event took place that was full of wonder. In that experience a bonding occurred. Many years later one of those men wrote a letter. The freshness of that event on the mountain, and the power of that bonding, were still evident, as the following paragraph from the letter shows.

We did not follow cleverly invented stories when we told you about the power and coming of our Lord Jesus Christ, but we were eye-witnesses of his majesty. For he received honor and glory from God the Father when the voice came to him from the Majestic Glory, saying, "This is my Son, whom I love; with him I am well-pleased." We ourselves heard this voice that came from heaven when we were with him on the sacred mountain (2 Peter 1:16-18, NIV).

There is something very beautiful to me about the way Peter says, ". . .*when we were with him* on the sacred mountain." Those words speak to me of a relationship. There are, perhaps, for each of us special times when we have been with Jesus in prayer, meditation, Bible study, or with his presence in another person. And a bonding took place each time that deepened the relationship, and increased our childlike faith, trust, wonder, and love.

THE CHILDREN
AROUND US—
WHO TEACH US
THE HEALING PROCESS

· T H I R T E E N ·

RESUMING TOUCH

hildren are up-front about their need for touch. One teacher who works in a school where breakfast is served told this story:

There is a little girl who comes to school to eat breakfast. I hugged her once and she started coming regularly. After about three weeks she said, "I don't come to breakfast to eat. The food's OK, but I come for the hugs—they're the only ones I get all day!"

Many adults have told how they have been released to touch through the touch of children. One person noted: "Children have taught me to hug—since *they* run up to me often with arms open wide."

A psychologist told of this freeing experience:

When I first started doing psychological testing with young children, I was struck by how open these young children (five to six) were. They used touch to express their feelings of warmth. It amazed me that they could feel warmth and affection with me in such a short time. Now I use touch with young children whom I am evaluating.

A teacher told how children helped her make the difficult transition from a long-established antiseptic, "touch-complex" life style to an open-to-touch-and-being-touched life style.

I learned to be more touching—to enjoy more physical contact. When I was younger I had a touch complex. But I found children to be so spontaneous, always tugging, touching, and hugging—that all of a sudden, I found myself doing the same thing. I know that in my first year of teaching when the children touched me I pulled back (inwardly). I don't know when it changed— I'm sure it took quite awhile.

■ TOUCH—A PEAK EXPERIENCE

Once in a while we have a single experience in touching/being touched that is so powerful that our lives are changed from that moment. One such experience was recounted by a new mother, who reported that she gained a sense of responsibility from that moment.

It wasn't until I was thirty-four that I was able to hold a child of my own in my arms. I will never forget the feeling. At first I was in such wonder, on a high, so terribly excited and happy. This was the greatest experience I'd ever had, and I had a wonderful man to share it with. We calmed down, thank goodness, and while I was still in the hospital, another very strong, emotional experience occurred. I don't really remember if it happened on the second or third day. I do remember it happening during the 4:00 A.M. feeding. I was sitting there nursing, looking at her, and suddenly it occurred to me that she was mine; I was going to take her home—and I felt this overwhelming sense of responsibility. I can't really elaborate much more because words don't seem to begin to be able to describe what happened. It wasn't really scary, just so strong.

■ TOUCH—A WAY TO MAKE IT THROUGH THE DAY

My own experience has taught me that touch helps me cope. One morning I was getting ready to leave the house to teach my eight o'clock class. For some reason I was furious with the entire world, including (especially) myself. I gave my wife a perfunctory Dagwood-Blondie exit kiss, but she caught me just outside the door and said, "I think you need a hug." That hug helped me enter my work day with a newfound serenity.

Children can also meet these survival needs of adults. They move as nurturers among adults. Many stories from adults contained statements like the following:

I learned from a child that a hug on a rough day makes that day seem not so rough after all.

No matter how bad a day I've been having at school, if a child comes up to me and gives me a hug, all my woes and troubles seem to disappear.

I've learned from a very special child that a smile and a hug can heal a sad moment.

■ TOUCH—AND DEPRIVATION

What happens when we are on a diet of regular touch, and that touching stops? We experience deprivation and sensory starvation. Most children go through some deprivation. They are touched totally in the womb. Then as an infant they are touched regularly (diapering, feeding, cuddling). As a little child, they are still very attractive to adults, and therefore continue to receive a great deal of touch. As older children, they may not be so attractive to adults, and therefore they get touched less. By the time they are in junior high school, many early adolescents rely on aggressive behavior (slapping a friend on the back, pushing, and shoving) to meet their needs for touch.

Adults can get a feel for this kind of loss if they have been to camps or conferences at which there was a great deal of touching and hugging, and then made the transition to an out-of-touch world. One adult talked about such a reentry problem:

While working at a summer camp in Colorado with nine-to-eleven-year-old girls I learned about a daily nutrient our body needs that we often neglect. Each day at camp I received tight-gripped hugs all day long from the girls. After leaving the mountains at the end of the summer, I went into a state of shock—lacking my daily hugs. Everyone knows adults aren't supposed to hug—how sad.

■ TOUCH—ASKING FOR IT
Since children are up-front about their need for touch we can learn from them to *ask* for touch. The child in the following story was able to request touch:

A child needs love to make it. I know a child that has a discipline problem. We told him to come to us for a hug when he feels he needs it instead of "acting up." It is working.

Perhaps we adults would not "act up" so much if we would say, "I need to be touched." A hug or kiss can be an effective remedy—or better yet, a potent preventive medicine—for yelling, hitting, or pouting.

The following story is an interesting illustration of how children place emphasis on action, while adults can get caught up in talking.

I've learned from children to show love to those closest to us! I was giving a devotional to a college-age group, talking about love and how the group was a place of love, when my daughter came up to me and nonverbally got my attention, looked me in the eye, pointed to herself, and indicated that she wanted a hug. Scripture teaches that we must be doers of the Word.

Most of the touch mentioned in this chapter has been hugging. That is because most of the stories having to do with touch were about hugging. However, just a little pat can be useful in bringing about renewed closeness in a relationship.

I have a niece named Mary Sue. She's two years old and talks very plainly and completely. She is being reminded constantly not to put such things as toothpicks in her mouth. One day my mom was baking a cake and chewing on a toothpick when Mary Sue suddenly noticed Grandma. She said, "Grandma, get that toothpick out of your mouth—it's NASTY!" Mom stood, holding her laugh, but within seconds Mary Sue patted Mom's leg and said, "Grandma, I'm sorry, I had to yell at you like that!"

By then both her mom and grandma had to laugh. But by this little incident I learned that some children realize that many times they are not yelled at to be punished or condemned, but in order to help them improve themselves. And even when they are yelled at and told the reasons why, apologies should follow.

Many other things happened in this story besides the pat on Grandma's leg. But the pat was important. Mary Sue used it to show her acceptance of her grandmother, even though she could not accept her behavior. At two years of age she was able to differentiate between the person and the problem and to communicate that understanding! We need to relearn these skills from the Mary Sues of our world.

· *F O U R T E E N* ·

AROUSING LAUGHTER

t Thanksgiving dinner in my family we always go around the table and say what we are thankful for. When my little sister was four, she said she was thankful she wasn't the turkey.

Sometimes it's funny when a child (or adult) simply makes a heartfelt comment on life, as the above four-year-old did. Children, who approach life in a straightforward way, are especially effective communicators.

■ LAUGHTER AND CHILDHOOD

It is a well-known fact that when a little child enters a room, many adults immediately become more cheerful. One reason children have this effect is that they are themselves optimistic, cheerful, and celebrating. Are adults, by nature, fun loving? Some children are concerned about this:

My five-year-old is afraid of only two things in life—getting baptized and growing up. We've talked a lot about growing up and it made me wonder what kind of image I'm presenting as an adult. She has expressed to me that she does not want to grow up because she is afraid she won't have any fun.

In order to keep laughter and the sense of humor alive in our adult lives, we will need to continue to be with and learn from children.

■ AROUSING THE PLAY INSTINCT

Sometimes children, or adults, begin smiling, playing, and laughing together. Before long *everything* is funny. They can't stop laughing. Norman Cousins calls hearty laughter such as this "internal jogging."[1] The arousal of the play instinct makes everything funnier. One adult told how her little sister made her aware of this:

I've learned that part of me will be six years old forever, and that's great! At times and places when I want to appear to be a mature college student, my little sister chooses to make faces at me. I then prove my maturity by making faces back, only I am usually the one who gets caught. This relaxes everybody and I know that things can only get better from there on.

There is something very therapeutic about being a part of escalating emotions. Sometimes the participants cannot sit still any longer. Simply laughing is not enough. They "roll in the aisles."

A dignified, poised woman told the following two stories about her grandson's ability to make adults lose their inhibitions and roll around on the floor:

My grandson and I were washing the patio door and he would put his tongue on the glass and make faces at me on the other side. I am amazed that he could suddenly make me lose all inhibitions and mimic him as he did me.

Our grandson loves to play ball. One day my husband and I engaged in a raucous game of ball with him. We were formal at first and played in an organized manner. Soon we began

*to laugh while he laughed, to yell, and to roll on the floor. All
at once we were rolling, tickling, and laughing together.*

■ **JOKING AND THE SENSE OF THE RIDICULOUS**
The following story confirms the fact that children's jokes
don't even have to be "funny" for adults to laugh at
them:

*We were on our way to see grandparents when my youngest
(about five) started telling jokes. This went on for at least half
an hour. They were all made up spontaneously, and they came
in rapid succession. He was laughing very hard at every joke.
Even though none made sense, we all laughed with him, and
that was like fuel that kept him going. Until then I was beginning
to worry about him, since he did not seem very sociable. That
seemed to have done it for him. We traveled a lot when the
children were little, and that remains a most memorable experience.*

Children's sense of humor apparently comes with them
as original equipment. One- and two-year-olds are already "clowning around":

*David, at twenty-seven months, was already making up jokes.
This one was completely on his own. I have no idea where it
came from. We were sitting at breakfast and David was waving
to all of us, when suddenly he looked up at me, smiled, and
said, "I didn't know pickles could wave." Obviously, it's not
a joke that is going to put the world in stitches, but I think it
is interesting that he could understand the concept of saying
something ridiculous to make people laugh. It helped us start
the day on a brighter note. A two-year-old can say anything
and be funny. Nothing cheers me up like hearing one of my
children have a good laugh. I always end up laughing, too.*

■ LAUGHTER AS A RELEASE

Laughter has been used for a long time as a release from pain. When a child has been hurt, adults will sometimes try to get the child to laugh in an attempt to prevent crying.

With our two grandsons being only a few weeks apart, it has been fun seeing the stages of development. The one that I missed noting in my own sons was the "laugh-out-loud" stage. I saw it in my grandsons because they both started doing it at our house. The older one was learning to toddle around the coffee table when he fell down. I said, "Kaboom," and up from him came that deep-down belly laugh of pure joy. A very similar situation happened with our younger grandson a few weeks later.

Laughter not only serves as a pain reliever, it can also provide a general release in our lives. The laughter of children is infectious because they go "all out" in this area just as they do in others.

Perhaps what I admire most in kids is their ability to approach things with total abandon. They really seem to get into what they are doing and into what is going on around them. I sometimes—really quite frequently—feel that I have lost much of this. My life is full with husband, child, work, school, and self—I often feel driven, that time passes without notice. I want to regain the wonder with which a child views life. If I think hard, I can remember what it was like to daydream, play make-believe, see shapes in the clouds, and try to catch a bird by putting salt on his tail. All of that was such wonderful fun.

This yearning adult is working toward the goal, as most of us are, of being released. Learning from children how to laugh can help in reaching that goal. Dr. Albert Schweitzer was apparently a "released," childlike adult.

Norman Cousins told of visiting the Schweitzer hospital at Lambarene:

Laughter at the dinner hour was probably the most important course. . . . At one meal, for example, Dr. Schweitzer reported to the staff that, "as everyone knows, there are only two automobiles within seventy-five miles of the hospital. This afternoon, the inevitable happened; the cars collided. We have treated the drivers for their superficial wounds. Anyone who has reverence for machines may treat the cars."

The next evening, he passed along the news that six baby chicks had been born to Edna the hen, who made her home near the dock. "It was a great surprise to me," he said solemnly. "I didn't even know she was that way."

. . .Humor at Lambarene was vital nourishment.[2]

As we become more released and revive our sense of humor, we also can become more nourishing and healing to those around us.

Being cheerful keeps you healthy. It is slow death to be gloomy all the time (Proverbs 17:22, TEV).

RECLAIMING SENSITIVITY

*T*he Lord told his disciples to become like little children, which certainly would require adults to learn from children. Yet when most of us learn something from a child, we are surprised: "It really seems a bit odd—a *child* taught me this."

I've been puzzled for some time as to why some adults learn from children and some don't. My present thinking is that such learning requires an expressive child and a humble adult. This pleasant combination makes things happen in this story:

It was Jeremy's first day in preschool. His family had moved to a new town after school was underway for one year. He found himself terrified and tongue-tied when the teacher asked him to talk during show-and-tell time. He stood, three and a half years old, silent, with twenty pairs of eyes on him. The teacher waited. Another three-and-a-half-year-old got up, walked over, stood by Jeremy, and said, "Mrs. Walker, you should leave Jeremy alone because this is his first day in school and he needs more time just to be shy." Mrs. Walker said later that she thought about it, decided he was right, and went on to the next child. As a humble, open adult, she learned to be more sensitive. The child, as her teacher, was sensitive to Jeremy's needs (and also found the courage to be his advocate).

This story raises the question: Do we as adults need training in sensitivity—or retraining? (I am using "sensitive" as in the dictionary definitions: "receptive to sense impressions" and "delicately aware of the attitudes and feelings of others. . ." *Webster's New Collegiate Dictionary.*) Perhaps it is sensitivity *retraining* that we adults need. The evidences indicate that young children are sensitive. The above preschool situation showed that a small child could be "delicately aware" of the feelings and emotional pain of another child.

■ AWARENESS OF CONFUSED FEELINGS

Many adults have told me they have learned to be sensitive to others' feelings because a child was sensitive to *their* feelings. Here is one example:

My husband was in an alcoholic treatment center. I was a wreck and couldn't make sense of all the emotions I was feeling. I was driving with my three-year-old in the back seat when I heard him singing a little made-up song, "My feelings are all mixed up. They're going 'round and 'round." I had been so caught up in my own struggle that I had not shared anything with him or asked him what he was feeling. I'm not even sure I could have expressed it as clearly.

Amazing sensitivity! Those of us who counsel could hope for such a keen sense of empathy.

■ AWARENESS OF THE NEED FOR EMOTIONAL SUPPORT

People need emotional support—affirmation and the confirmation that they are worthwhile and loved—just as they need food. Moreover, just as there are times when people are especially hungry for food, so there are times when they are famished for emotional support. Children sense this need. Their *timing* in giving such support is too accurate to be the result of chance.

I am a single parent. One day I was very ill with the flu. I was feeling pretty sorry for myself because I felt all alone. Here I was, really too sick to look after myself, let alone my six-year-old son. I needed someone to care for me! My son came over to the couch, gave me a big hug and kiss, and said, "I'll take care of you, Mom." Just what I needed to hear.

This six-year-old sensed the need of his mother for emotional support from a care-giver. He became that care-giver and gave her the needed support.

■ CHILDREN—KEEN OBSERVERS

How do children *sense* others' feelings? Note the following adult's viewpoint on this:

I baby-sat for my cousin one summer, and he realized I was upset that day, so he came up to me and said he was sorry and gave me a hug and an "I love you." He was two-and-a-half years old and he wasn't the reason for my being upset. Children know when their parent or someone else is upset and they can sense the tension. I feel children don't want to hurt anyone, so they say they're sorry even though it wasn't their fault. It made me feel very good inside and I tried to get over things that bothered me before I went to baby-sit. Kids are good observers and their innocence shows they care about you and your feelings.

The babysitter's belief that children are good observers coincides with that of the following adult:

I've learned how important my face and voice are in conveying emotion. My child knows when I'm happy, sad, mad, etc., more by my face and tone than by any words. So, I guess he also knows when I'm proud, disappointed, etc., too, without my ever saying a word.

■ SENSITIVITY TO INNER QUALITIES

Children and adults are sensitive—to different things. This is one of the themes of the book, *The Little Prince*.

If you were to say to the grown-ups: "I saw a beautiful house made of rosy brick, with geraniums in the windows and doves on the roof," they would not be able to get any idea of that house at all. You would have to say to them: "I saw a house that cost $20,000." Then they would exclaim: "Oh, what a pretty house that is!"[1]

And the little prince goes on to say of adults, "They are like that. One must not hold it against them. Children should always show great forbearance toward grown-up people."[2]

The little prince saw a special beauty in a house that the adults did not see. Perhaps in the same way the child in the following story saw a special beauty in a person that the adults did not see:

I had a four-year-old in preschool who was a real "pistol." He would sit through activities designed to get out the "wigglies," would scribble on other children's papers, but not on his own, etc. I really wondered how he'd react to a visit to a nursing home on May Day. He was extraordinarily kind, especially when directed to an old lady whose face looked quite grotesque. This little boy, instead of saying something unkind, seemed to sense her need for his special kind of caring. He walked right up to her bed, took her hand, and said, "Hi, I'm Ken! Who are you?" The lady sparkled with delight.

FORGIVING

any parents have learned from their children about that most perplexing subject in the curriculum of life—forgiveness. This parent had a master teacher:

When big sister was disciplined for hurting little sister, big sister cried for her blanket (the special one that comforts her). I didn't let her have it for a few minutes, so little sister, who had just been hurt by big sister, went and brought her the blanket.

■ FRESHNESS
One prerequisite for facing the world fresh every day is a forgiving spirit. If we do not adopt forgiveness as a life style, we will gradually shoulder a larger and larger burden of resentments and bitterness, and life will become heavy—and stale. We will breathe the old air of anger or pouting as we rehearse mentally every day the injustices done to us. I once heard a pastor say to another pastor who had suffered an injustice, "Don't brood over it." Brooding robs us of the joy and freshness of living.

Jesus faced every day with freshness because he forgave. This freshness can also be seen in children before they become "adulterated." Little children have flashes of anger, but they don't "carry a grudge." It is the *carrying* of a grudge that takes away the vitality and freshness of life. How can we regain a forgiving spirit, and thus be helped to live an uncluttered, simple, renewed life?

■ LEARNING FROM CHILDREN TO FORGIVE IMMEDIATELY

We live in a world of instant coffee, fast foods, and crash diets. We want it *now*. But who is pushing instant forgiveness, fast reconciliation, and a crash method of forgetting grudges? The Lord—and children. This adult learned from her own childhood about instant forgiveness:

Adults should learn to forgive and forget as easily as children do. My mother tells a story about when I was a child. I came in crying and saying that my little friend had hit me. Mom comforted me and told me not to go back, but to stay with her. There was a knock at the door. My friend wanted to play. Mom said I jumped from her lap, full of smiles and ready to play again.

Can you remember, as the above adult did, a time when forgiveness came fast and did not even require an apology? Forgiving someone does not mean that we forget the incident which originated the grudge. Rather, it means that we open our hands and let go of the grudge. I can think of a man for whom I held bitterness for over a year. (I have not been a model of instant forgiveness!) When forgiveness came, I first realized it when I saw him one day and the venom didn't flood through my body. Now as I remember the incident which embittered me, I have forgotten what the emotion felt like! I can no longer recall (bring back) the feelings of animosity and meanness toward that man. FREEDOM!

Here are some other stories from adults who have learned about rapid forgiveness from children:

I've learned that children forgive readily and don't hold grudges for long. My own children taught me this as I am sometimes cross, unreasonable, preoccupied, and impatient with them.

Our nine-year-old has taught me about forgiveness and renewal. He bounces out of bed at 6:45 A.M. Then he takes his shower, dresses, and is ready to meet the new day. Yesterday is forgotten. What exists is today.

I've learned how easy it is to forgive. Sean and I can be so mad at each other. He is so obnoxious sometimes, and stubborn and rude, and finally I will send him to his room. The other day was like that, and as we got to his room, he blew up at me and let it all out. As soon as he was done he hugged me and we could forgive each other completely. It seems that with adults the anger hangs on so much longer.

■ WITHHOLDING FORGIVENESS "FOR THE OTHER PERSON'S GOOD"

An insightful story dealt with a universal issue—one that most of us have grappled with for a long time. It is possible to harbor an unforgiving spirit and at the same time believe we are doing the other person a good turn:

When I yield to anger after having just resolved never to verbalize those angry feelings again, I then promptly ask my child to forgive me, anxiously awaiting, "That's OK, Mommy." However, if she asks for forgiveness too quickly after a repeated offense, I've sometimes felt a need to hold back my forgiveness in order to teach a lesson. "After all," I reason, "she needs to realize the seriousness of this spilt milk."

The above story spotlights an often unrecognized stumblingblock to forgiveness—the need to "teach a lesson" to the other person. It is as if we were doing the other person a favor by withholding immediate forgiveness. Many of us have learned, by the time we are adults, a "suffering" view of education: Teaching is punitive and learning is painful.

That is the implicit idea behind the statement, "There! That will teach you a lesson!" or, "I sure taught him a lesson!" But little children have positive beliefs about education. To them learning is fun and exciting. So they teach us the principle of immediate forgiveness by *doing* it.

The lessons that another adult learned regarding forgiveness have stayed with her for over twenty years. And the relationship with the child who taught her has continued all those years.

Many years ago I learned that a child has an unlimited spirit of forgiveness and love. One of my third-grade students was failing to get his assignments completed by class time or even by the end of the day. Finally, I decided as a last resort to keep this child in after school each afternoon until the work was completed. To my dismay, he worked just as slowly after school as he did during the day.

I kept on prodding him daily as my patience was getting shorter and shorter. He would continue to look up with a big smile. We both continued to endure it, and at last he did get his work completed and managed to keep up each day. He had lost out on many activities, but smiled right through it.

Now this boy is an adult and has children of his own. He wears the same smile as he did so many years ago. When we meet on the street and stop to have a friendly chat, this incident of his school years sometimes comes up and we both have a good laugh.

And probably that is the most important thing about forgiveness—it allows a relationship to continue!

· S E V E N T E E N ·

DISCOVERING—
WITH A CHILD'S HELP—
HOW TO MOURN

Somewhere in our growing-up days, many of us have learned to bury our sadness, to bottle up our sorrows. Jesus said, "Happy are those who mourn; God will comfort them!" (Matthew 5:4, TEV). How do we become *able* to mourn *again?* Children have a great deal to teach us about expressing sorrow. A little child can cry, even wail. A college student told me this story about how, at a time when she was experiencing grief from a breakup, a child helped her to mourn:

One of my little cousins (four years old) was with me one day, and wanted to know what was wrong. So I told her what was wrong and she said, "Why don't you just cry?" I don't know if she had heard it from somebody or came up with it by herself, but it sure helped me.

This adult found herself crying—mourning—because a child had asked an elegantly simple question and thereby released her. Being able to mourn saves our body. According to Montagu, the body *will* weep, whether we shed tears or not:

Meanwhile, his repressed weeping may be somatized, that is, expressed through the body, either in weeping through the skin in various eruptions, through the gastrointestinal tract in colitis or ulcers, through the respiratory tract in asthmatoid conditions, or in various other neurogenic symptoms.[1]

Happiness really does come to those who mourn. This story illustrates in more detail how the process works:

I keep thinking of the time when my fiancé was working out of town. He had been gone for over a month. It was getting near Christmas and my birthday, but I was not in the mood at all because I was feeling alone and depressed.

I work with children who are eighteen months to three years old. I was sitting in a chair holding a child, and I was feeling sad and had tears in my eyes. The child I was holding asked me, "What's the matter?" I said, "I'm just sad." The little boy said, "Why are you sad? I love you." I cried and held the child close. From that day on I was in the Christmas mood.

This adult was able to move in a few minutes' time from grieving or mourning to celebrating. What made the difference? The intervention of a caring child.

Children are skilled comforters, and being comforted can help us mourn.

I learned that children are great comforters, that they accept death more easily. When my grandmother died three years ago, it was my children who comforted me rather than vice versa. Their assurances were that Grandma was with Jesus; that God had things in control. I would not have accepted these assurances or been comforted nearly as much had an adult been trying to comfort me. It was a beautiful experience. I was comforted!

Why was this adult more receptive to comfort from children than she would have been from adults? Perhaps because adults are "expected" to give comfort, while children are not. Perhaps, also, because children may have greater skills in giving comfort.

Two years ago, I went through the death of my father. My husband and I worked with my son for a year so he would know that his grandfather was dying. We were hoping that when Grandpa died I would not have to respond to my son's needs as well as my own. We knew that at this time I would have difficulty handling my own emotions. When Grandpa did die, the neatest thing happened. For awhile I did lose control of myself, and my son stepped in at that point to help me. It was as though he understood everything. He put his arms around me and patted me on the back. He kept telling me, "It's all right, Mommy! Grandpa loves you. He is in heaven and he can see you." Everything I had told him was coming back to me. It was a real comfort.

He was three when we found out that my dad was dying. I feel that if anyone has helped me to accept the death of my dad, it has been my son with his understanding of death. Even though this probably doesn't seem like very much—for me it was enough.

This three-year-old:

> was sensitive to his mother's "loss of control"
> took the initiative
> hugged and patted
> communicated in some way that he understood
> continued his comfort-giving ("He *kept* telling me. . .")
> used what he had been taught about comforting
> was effective ("For me it was enough")

Children can teach adults, through their example, to receive comfort—even to seek it. One child was able to communicate to an adult her great pain and to receive comfort so her mourning could begin:

I remember the time one little girl came to preschool. She looked so sad that morning. I leaned down to her eye level, and smiled at her and said, "Good morning." She said, "Teacher, my mommy and daddy are getting a divorce." She threw her arms around me and hugged me so tight. I found it was not necessary to use words to comfort her. Just holding her in my arms was all the communication that was needed. Sometimes we feel we always have to use words. Many times just being there is enough.

Another way that children can help adults work through the grieving process is by reminding the adults to trust the Lord:

When my mother died, my children ranged in age from ten to a baby. As we explained death to them and what had happened to Grandma, I talked about the joy and happiness we should have about death. So everything went fine, until one day my son, age nine, came in and found me crying and he said, "Why are you crying, Mom?" I told him I was thinking of Grandma, and not to worry; it was OK. He said something I'll never forget, "But, Mom, if we are supposed to be so happy for Grandma, why cry?" Of course I went ahead to explain that sometimes we cry for ourselves more than for the one who has died. But I think so often, when I am asking my children to live a life of trust in God, am I also living that life?

Children are good at reminding adults of the obvious. And it is the obvious for which we need reminders: the need to express love, to affirm others, to give and receive touch, to sing and move and play, and to trust God. It is a gift from God to be reminded of a need which is so close to us we cannot see it.

Kent Estes, my partner in this study on learning from children, helped me understand that a newborn infant can be a very positive factor in the grieving/healing process. Some years ago when Kent's mother was dying, his wife was pregnant with their first child. During this time of letting go of one life and taking hold of another, Kent wrote the following poem:

THE DEATH OF MY MOTHER   THE BIRTH OF MY SON

Thoughts of a Family Journey
(Oct. 1977—Dec. 1978)

Hello, Dad, Mom—cancer,
  my God!

Anger, fear, despair—
I'm not ready for this.

How do you prepare? Maybe you
  don't.
Maybe you find a friend—that's it.
Someone to talk to.
I know just what you're going
  through. . . .
If I hear one more cancer story
  I'll. . . .
Why won't they listen to me?

If cure is the only hope—there's no
  hope—but it's not!

Priorities—what's really
  important?
Death! Inevitable.

Love—letting be, letting go—
  alone.

The pain! It's over.
Death—a going on.
  It amazes me!

Hello, Doc, Barb—a baby,
  my God!

Apprehension, fear, excitement—
I'm not ready for this.

How do you prepare? Maybe you
  don't.
Maybe you find a friend—that's
  it.
Someone to talk to.
It's more than everything you can
  imagine—
more demanding, rewarding,
  joyful, frustrating.
It's simply more important. . . .
That helps, thanks for telling me.

The birth of a baby, an assurance
  that the world must go on!

Priorities—what's really
  important?
Life! Inescapable.

Love—making contact, letting
  in—together.

The pain! It's over.
Birth—a beginning.
  It amazes me!

Kent Estes

FINDING HELP FOR BROKENNESS

n many of our stories children have appeared in the role of healers of parents. Some parents, like the mother mentioned below, were helped to recover from hurt feelings:

While watching his mother softly shed a tear or two, her three-year-old son asked Mommy why she was sad. She replied that the lady who had just left had hurt her feelings. He asked if she took all the good ones away. Not understanding what he meant, the mother asked him to explain. He repeated, "Did she take all your good ones away?" The mother asked, "Do you mean good feelings?" A nod of the head started the mother to realizing that he was feeling her sadness and identifying with her frustration of one minute being happy and then turning to tears. He came up to her and said, "I like you, Mommy, bunches and bunches!" The mother felt healed.

Some of the stories are funny, even though the child involved was serious.

Here is a young would-be counselor:

A twenty-eight-month-old boy heard his fourteen-month-old brother crying. He went into the next room where his brother was and said, "Daniel, do you want to talk about your problem?"

Probably one of the most healing things a child can do for us is to teach us to be childlike:

In one house where we lived, the little neighbor girl, who was about three or four years old, used to love to come over and see me. Somehow, she helped me emotionally cope with my adopted teenagers.

She always seemed to come over when I was bored or when I was depressed or angry about something, and she always cheered me up. I loved to talk to her because she took me out of my hypocrisy and the drain of being forced to be an adult all the time. Just picking her up and carrying her did so much for me.

The child cheered up her neighbor by releasing her to be real and not to have to "act adult."

■ RESTORERS OF THE SPIRIT
What does a schoolteacher do who senses a need for healing? She goes and plays with a child:

Children have really ministered to me over the years in a lot of ways—whether I'm up, really feeling good, or feeling low. At these extreme times of my emotions, I really enjoy being around children.

When I was teaching school there was a family that lived near me, and whenever I felt lonely I would go there knowing that I would be accepted and loved openly. Children are open and genuine, and willing to accept and receive, and to give so much love, too, in return. And there are so many times that I have not known how to relate to an adult, but I knew that I just needed someone to care. Children supply that for me.

Now, if I am coming home from teaching school all day, and I'm frustrated or down, it's really neat to be able to go by my sister's house and to play with my niece. It's so encouraging and uplifting. There's something about the lighthearted joy of a child that restores my spirit.

Here are the healing qualities of children mentioned by this teacher:

ministering
accepting
loving
open
genuine
receiving
giving
caring
playful
encouraging
uplifting
joyful
restorers of the spirit

Restorers of the spirit! That's an accurate summary of the healing ministry of children. One three-year-old began this restoring process with her grieving mother:

I learned a deeper meaning of God's caring from my daughter who was three at the time. I had just lost my mother—a young mother in my opinion, fifty-six years of age. Although I had the assurance that she was in God's presence, I went through tremendous grief and had a terrible sense of loss. On one occasion I had heard some music which touched me deeply. My daughter saw me crying. She came and put her arms around me and said, "Mama, someone wants to talk to you on the phone [she handed me her play telephone]. It's Jesus and he wants to tell you he's taking good care of Nana." At that moment I believe some healing took place in my heart.

■ THE HEALING OF KATHY

Kathy's journey through brokenness has been a painful one, including sexual assault as a child, frequent depressions, an overdose, anxiety attacks, withdrawal into aloneness and loneliness, sexual assault as an adult, and periods of doubt—doubts about God, doubts about her own worth.

Now, at age twenty-one, she is in a different place spiritually and psychologically than she was just two years ago. There is a sense of wholeness and radiance about her. She is more confident, more able to give love, and more released and free. She has experienced—and is continuing to experience—healing. Much of her healing has come through children. She agreed to tell her story of these healing experiences.

The first incident that comes to mind is when I was going to baby-sit over at my friends' house. They have two little kids, Melanie and Mark. I had never heard Mark speak a word. He's about two years old and he's a late talker. I didn't feel like baby-sitting that night because I just felt rejected and I was really depressed. The little kids wanted me to go outside and play with them. I told them, "Well, could you wait a minute? I'd like to stay inside and just pray. I'm not feeling real well." Melanie asked me if it would be OK if she prayed with me. I was sitting at the kitchen table and she came up and sat down in the chair beside me and put her elbows on the table; and Mark came running over and stood in between Melanie and me, and she said, "Dear God, please make Kathy feel better. Amen." And she nudged Mark and he said, "Amen." That made me laugh. I didn't feel my rejection anymore. For the rest of the night and a couple of days I was just tickled pink.

A couple who were friends of mine have four little kids. They always wanted me to baby-sit, and if the kids heard my name they'd go, "All right!" It made me feel really accepted. And the

*four-year-old just fell in love with me, so everywhere I went
she would follow me.*

*And there would be a lot of times when I'd go over there
after church and sit down, and she would crawl up into my
lap. She was a real cuddly little thing, and she'd just fall asleep
in my arms and my depression would leave. So I used to love
to go over there. Every time I get depressed I like to hold little
kids. I don't know, there's something in that.*

*A number of times I was starting to feel really down about myself
because I felt like I was about ready to fall spiritually.
And I'd go to lead an evening girls' group at church, and it
never failed. The girls would come up to me. They'd either hug
me, or it would be an exciting thing for them that they got to
sit by me. It just made me feel like I was OK. I could see Jesus
in them.*

*I never felt I was very responsible, but because they believed
that I was responsible, and because of their childlike way of
enjoying me, it always made me feel, "I can be responsible."
Or, when I didn't feel I was doing a very good job, they always
thought of me as doing a good job. I started doing things. I
was on time because I knew if I didn't get there the kids would
have to stand out in the cold, or they'd be running around the
building screaming, and I just knew that I had to be there. I
knew I was needed.*

*One morning I was sitting with the group of girls in church
and I sensed the Lord was prompting me to ask for prayer.
So I stood up and I asked all the little girls who were around
me to pray for me. And the Lord did a lot of ministering to
me through that . . . humbling me. I felt humbled having little
girls praying for me. But yet in another way, I felt very priv-
ileged; and God told me through their praying that he was going
to fuse my past, present, and future together . . . like a river.
God used their prayer to show me that my life was going to be
flowing as one stream—not stagnant. And that was a big
healing time.*

I've also worked with foster homes, and seeing children who were abused or hurt just made me feel terrible. *But there was something about them, the way they knew they would make it through. They hadn't decided yet that they* weren't *going to make it. They gave me courage and strength to go on in a lot of ways. And it gave me some ways to go back into my childhood at that point when those things were happening to* me. *I would give them advice, and it was like I was healing myself through that.*

I guess I've gone from one place to a completely different place, and a lot of the reason is children. It has been a slow, healing process.

A little girl in the group was being rejected by all the other girls. She reminds me a lot of me when I was little; and at first it was really hard for me to work with her because that part of me hurt. People would say we even looked alike, and that didn't make it any better. She's only nine, and she and her girl friends stand out in the street and try to hitchhike. Then, if a car stops, they stand there and talk to the people. This is very dangerous, *and it reminds me a lot of the chances I took as a kid. She concerns me a lot.*

She is only in fourth grade, and she was apparently assaulted as a child; I was also sexually assaulted. She has some weird reactions when men come around, behavior that reminds me of the way I reacted. And I've talked with her about that; but to see how young *she was as a fourth-grader and how little her body is, relieved my guilt over the time when I was a child. I have felt for a long time like it was my fault. And to look at her complete lack of understanding of sexual things freed that part of my life—released me from that guilt. That was a BIG healing time for me.*

It's great to watch children play and learn about what's new in the world, and to see how excited they are by little things— when I get so bogged down by the whole world's problems. I get on my knees and get down into their lives, and I look closely and see that the cupboard door is fascinating, or that the car-peting has so many different colors in it. This brings me down to earth and my problem doesn't seem so big. Doing these things, and also holding kids, helps my depression. And seeing me in kids heals my past—seeing kids that were like me. Kids who weren't as fortunate or maybe more fortunate. I can see that they have the same struggles. That I wasn't abnormal. God has done a lot of healing in my life!

How did the children serve as channels for God's heal-ing of Kathy? They:

> prayed for her
> accepted her
> let themselves be held by her
> hugged her
> chose her
> respected her
> expected her to be responsible
> believed in her
> understood her
> gave her a sense of the unity of life
> modeled resilience and courage
> talked with her
> accepted her as a part of their (play) group

All these things which the children did for Kathy are things the Lord does for us. Jesus prays for us, accepts us, chooses us, respects us, etc. So the children had ministered to Kathy in the place of Jesus. And that is what brought healing to her.

As I listened to Kathy's audio-tape from which the above transcript was made, I thanked God for the clear evidences of her healing. I know where she was two years ago, and I know where she is now. I'm convinced Kathy is a survivor. She is humble, open, nondefensive, trusting, creative, vulnerable, and loving. She has, in fact, become childlike to the extent that she is able to "get down on all fours" and see the world as a child sees it. And being on eye level with children, she has been able to see them along her path, signaling to her the way out of brokenness into wholeness.

THE CHILDREN
AROUND US—
WHO TEACH US GROWTH
AS A WAY OF LIFE

LEARNING TO MOVE, PLAY, AND SING—AGAIN

I suppose the greatest impact on me from my two-year study of how adults learn from children has been the dawning awareness that *movement is the natural state of life.* This has been a shocking, painful realization to a sedentary college professor, requiring a careful reappraisal of my life style.

The questions flood in as I observe children:

Won't they ever stop moving?
Where do they get their energy?
Perhaps they'll slow down soon?
Why isn't moving around as much fun for me as it is for them?
Is the fun only in *what* they are doing, or is it also in the movement itself?

■ MOVING TO MUSIC

Dancing, an ancient art form, begins very young. Almost as soon as children learn to walk, they begin to dance. In fact, one child was reported to have begun dancing on the very day he learned to walk.

My great-nephew learned to walk on his first birthday, and that was the day he also danced to the music he heard on the commercials. He was so funny. He danced in one place, but kept time with the beat. In a week he had learned to dance by going around and around until he fell over. Then he'd clap his hands, get up, and dance again.

My daughter, Sue, noted that both her children began to dance when they were about the same age:

At a very young age (right around a year) both of our boys began to dance in response to music. Sometimes it's in time with the music, but more often it isn't. Sometimes it consists of just bouncing up and down, and often it means running and jumping. Once I got out some scarves and we danced and swayed with our scarves in time to the music. Sometimes David will say, "Dance with me!" Sometimes their dancing includes touching another person, like holding hands, but that is more often an adult's idea. They usually dance alone. However, the call is still there, though unspoken, and I usually find myself swaying with them where I am, if not getting up and joining in the dance.

Dance with me! When that invitation comes from a child, it's very difficult to resist, as some "inhibited" college students discovered.

I attended a Bible school that encouraged students to be expressive in their worship; nevertheless, some of us remained traditionally inhibited during our chapel services. On one occasion, the nursery was closed and parents brought their young children to the service. Their immediate response to the songs of praise was to clap, jump, and dance excitedly in the aisles back in a far corner of the auditorium. Jesus' admonition to become as little children was inescapably evident in their joyous celebration of praise. Many of us joined them in the aisles that day, experiencing for the first time the pure joy of uninhibitedly praising the Lord.

The celebration in the aisles of the college chapel that day must have been similar to that spontaneous celebration which occurred when King David brought the ark of the covenant to Jerusalem:

David and all the Israelites were dancing and singing with all their might to honor the Lord. They were playing harps, lyres, drums, rattles, and cymbals (2 Samuel 6:5, TEV).

Children can call us to a spontaneous expression of worship by movement if their participation in church is permitted and encouraged. Benson and Stewart argue for the presence of children in church worship as full participants, and, at times, as leaders.[1]

■ WORKING AND PLAYING

What are the differences between work and play? Here are some ways to view those differences:

WORK—Concentrate on the *product.*
PLAY—Concentrate on the *process.*
WORK—The important thing is the *destination.*
PLAY—The important thing is the *journey.*
WORK—Is for the *future.*
PLAY—Is in the *now.*
WORK—Another person's *play.*
PLAY—Another person's *work.*

Obviously, both work and play are important, and play is beginning to get better press with adults. One of the nation's leading educational organizations recently devoted an entire issue of its research newsletter to play. In that research bulletin, twelve benefits of children's play were mentioned, as summarized by Jerome L. Singer. Among those benefits listed are:

sheer fun
persistence
self-entertainment and waiting ability
working through conflict
leadership and cooperation
resistance to television addiction[2]

These outcomes of play are just as beneficial to adults as to children. Note that several of these outcomes (especially sheer fun!) resulted from the playtimes that these two adults reported having with their children:

When my daughter was about two, we bounced up and down on the bed together. I can't remember why or how it started. But it was one of the things she enjoyed doing—bouncing around on our bed as if it were her trampoline. She seemed overjoyed that I had entered her world. My wife managed to get the camera out and capture this joyous moment for us to remember.

I had a fun time this summer trying to get our daughter over her fear of jumping into the pool and going down the slide in swimming lessons. We went to the pool and went through everything together. We started at three feet and went up to seven feet. Then the slide—I had more fun going down the water slide. When she saw me laughing and enjoying it, she decided to give it a try and found it to be delightful. We spent the rest of the day laughing and going down the slide together.

Adults who enrolled in the Learning from Children class talked about their reasons for enrolling. Some wanted to learn to play. One such person noted:

Personally, I am a very serious, intense, work- and production-oriented person. I have a hard time justifying "play" in my schedule. I am trying to find a happy balance between accepting myself as I am, and changing, in order to have more times of relaxation and fun. This is a personal growth goal for this course.

Another class member discussed the *riskiness* of becoming playful:

I have learned that relationships can be improved if I am willing to take risks in the course of improving them. I found it personally risky to allow myself to become more childlike, especially in the area of playfulness. I took a risk and tried it with my children, and I am a changed person. I still have a long way to go, but I have hope that my childlike traits will emerge and that relationships with children, particularly my own, will continue to improve.

"I took a risk and tried it [playfulness] with my children, and I am a changed person." That is a powerful statement about growth, since growth is positive change.

■ SINGING

Song is an international language, indeed. It is also very contagious. . . . Children have taught me to hum and sing while we work—learning cutting skills, puzzles, etc. Besides learning music, rhyming, language, etc., we're in unity through song!

Another adult found spiritual excitement under the teaching of her grandchild:

When our youngest grandson was only three years old, he sang for us a song he learned at church school, "I will sing of the mercies of the Lord forever." Although he may not have known the full meaning of the words, he had the exuberance and excitement that I had at times almost lost. He gave me a new excitement in remembering God's mercies.

Excitement is a common theme that runs through the moving, dancing, playing, and singing of children. Children can teach us to be excited again!

CREATING

etty Edwards has written an unusual textbook for college art courses, *Drawing on the Right Side of the Brain*.[1] She has experienced unusual success in bringing her students to drawing proficiency very rapidly. Her method is a simple one—she has her students focus on what they see, rather than thinking about (assigning words to) what they see. To do this she may turn the stimulus drawing upside down, or she may ask students to draw the space around the stimulus form. By using these methods, she has helped her students make amazing progress in just a few months' time in the accurate production of portraits. Dr. Edwards found that the shift in method was not easy to bring about with many students. It involved being released from words, to *see* forms and shapes.

Now, something like this is involved in being released to see the world as a child sees it. For example, note below how the child's lack of words helps produce a statement which provides a clear visual image:

I had a four-year-old girl who came to my daycare center every morning at 8:00. One morning her mother had to go to work at 7:00, so she brought her at 6:45. When she walked in, she said to me, "Teacher, the sun isn't working this morning."

The four-year-old reported what she "saw" rather than giving an analysis of the event. This direct way of interacting with their world apparently also allows children to see what isn't there—namely, a pretend world.

■ PRETENDING
Some adults reported learning from children who pretended. One felt enriched:

Pretending can give you the world! A little boy was visiting me and we were talking and playing. He stood on my porch and acted as if he was fishing, pulling on the pole and even showing through expressions that he was really fishing. Or think of little girls playing tea parties. If kids don't have something, they pretend. I learned that imagination is great!

A father was moved by his daughter's ability to pretend:

One Sunday before Christmas I told a class of three-and-a-half to four-and-a-half-year-olds the story of the Wise Men bringing gifts to baby Jesus. Then we wrapped individual boxes in gift paper and ribbon and filled them with love. One father came to the door to get his child at the close of the session and she handed him her own wrapped gift and said, "Daddy, this is for you." He opened it and, of course, he could see nothing. She exclaimed, "Daddy, it's full of love!" He kissed her. This was a very touching experience for me—especially since our holiday is filled with so many material gifts.

Children, of course, bring reality to their pretend world. That's why it's so powerful. The box *was* full of love to the four-year-old, and perhaps to the adult as well.

Reality, after all, often depends on one's point of view, as the following story illustrates:

I've learned to look at commonplace things with a sense of wonder and awe. Yesterday a stray dog wandered onto our farm. To me it was a smelly, mangy, flea-bitten mutt. To my boys it was a gift from God, a precious animal. They had him named in an hour.

■ CREATING BEAUTY

This adult was able, at least in retrospect, to appreciate her daughter's creation.

Our youngest daughter was probably two or less when on a windy day in Kansas she discovered an exciting game called "Flying Kleenex." Looking out the kitchen window, I saw Kleenex flying all over the neighborhood. On closer examination I found the original source—Sue was holding them up one at a time and letting the wind blow them out of her little hand. Our entire family went on a three- or four-block chase, gathering up as many as we could catch. I could see how much fun this was for her—something like blowing bubbles—or like creating an ever-changing pink sculpture series against the backgrounds of our neighbors' green yards and the blue sky. However, I'm not sure the neighbors appreciated the spectacular beauty of the event.

There are many evidences in our stories that children appreciate the beauty around them. The story of the two-year-old and the pink Kleenex shows that children are also interested in creating beauty. Children can teach adults, who have a similar urge, to *express* that urge. From our teenage years on, many of us become spectators of the visual and performing arts. We need the confidence to become participatory—to draw and paint, and to play an instrument and sing.

■ CREATIVITY AND THE DELAY OF CLOSURE

Robert Strom has noted that children delay closure:

Parents have a greater need than children do for reaching conclusions, and this accounts in part for parental frustration during play. Whereas the child moves from one focus to another and back again without revealing a need for completion, parents feel tension unless the play themes reach some type of conclusion.[2]

He notes further that parents, as well as children as young as nine or ten, show a preoccupation with rules. Little children for whom the delight is in the play rather than the outcome spend little time with rules. Strom has a concern in this area:

The more completion-conscious we become as a society, the less likely it is that we will be able to tolerate delayed closure when we meet this characteristic in children. However, the stubborn fact remains that creativity and the ability to delay closure go together.[3]

What can we learn from children in this area of creativity? Delaying closure is very helpful in discovering truth or in finding new ways of doing things. Using a playful approach in gathering information can often be valuable. Finally, if we don't need rules for a given situation, we should not make them.

■ CREATIVE ALTERNATIVES

A one-and-a-half-year-old "rodeo cowboy" needed to create a release chute for his bucking bronco. Here is his amazing creation:

The thing that comes to my mind is learning a sense of creativity from a child. My neighbor boy placed himself on his rolling horse and came riding into the kitchen. He went to the corner where he could open two cabinet doors so they touched back to back, creating a stall for a bronco. He would slam open the "gates," as it were, and ride the horse to the middle of the kitchen until he was bucked off. He figured out how to do this at a year-and-a-half by watching rodeos on TV. I was impressed at how creative he could be.

Another child came up with a creative alternative to buying a pet:

My eight-year-old daughter was begging for a pet after her sister got a gerbil. One night she came to me and said, "Don't get me a pet. It's more fun wanting one."

How does a blind child encounter God's creation? This calls for a creative alternative. A woman tells of a baby-sitting experience years ago which she cannot forget. Having read it, neither can I:

When I was a freshman in college I began baby-sitting for a three-year-old blind child. One time while I was at his house, he asked me to go outside with him and listen to the wind. His request really gave me something to think about and learn from.

■ THE ULTIMATE CREATIVE ALTERNATIVE
A teacher was trying to arbitrate one of those disagreements that occurs—repeatedly—in classrooms. In the process she learned something.

One morning two small boys were fighting over a little plastic man. I went over and tried to talk to them about sharing. It wasn't going so well. Another child walked over and gave one of the boys his plastic toy and all was settled. This little boy was able to show sharing when all I could do was try to tell about it.

The boy who intervened actually had several alternatives available. He could have:

done nothing
taken the side of one of the boys
initiated a disagreement with someone else while
the teacher was busy

Instead, he chose the ultimate creative alternative—
LOVE. This option is always available to us. Adults can
go to children to observe this creative choice, but children
can also learn from adults, as the following story (one of
my own) illustrates:

Kent and I were meeting with about ten teachers on
Friday at 6:45 A.M. We were part of their support group
that met regularly.

I asked a second-grade teacher, Sara (who is a childlike
adult), about a little plastic box she had with her. It was
full of necklaces from her growing-up days. Sara told this
story: She had a girl in her class who had asked her some
weeks previously if she had a bracelet from her childhood
days she would be willing to give away. Sara gave her a
bracelet. Then she asked if she had a ring. Sara gave her
a ring. Then she asked Sara if she had any necklaces. I
asked Sara if she was going to let the girl choose one of
the necklaces from the box. She replied that she was
going to give all of them to her!

At a later time when Kent and I met with the group,
she told the sequel to the story. The girl did not ask for
anything else. Also, an amazing thing was happening to
the class. They were all sharing and giving each other
prized possessions. Also, Sara had just had a birthday,
and one of the second-grade boys came up to her desk,
emptied his pockets of seventeen cents—all the money
he had—and said, "This is for your birthday."

Today is Easter. I am reminded of Jesus, who exer-
cised the ultimate creative alternative of love, and gave
all that he had—his life.

TWENTY-ONE

THINKING—THE CURIOUS CHILD

*L*earning from children *how to learn*—and even to recapture or resurface the *desire* to learn—can be an area of exciting surprises. When Norman Cousins was editor of *The Saturday Review of Literature,* he asked a number of famous people to respond to the question, "What have I learned?" Here is part of Albert Einstein's response to the question:

Pay close attention to the curiosities of a child; this is where the search for knowledge is freshest and most valuable.[1]

An adult who has a very close, warm relationship with her eight-year-old niece, Angie, reported this conversation as an illustration of a child's curiosity, and the desire to experience all of life's joys:

Angie: "Is it fun being married?"
Aunt: "Well—yes."
Angie: "I mean, is it fun to sleep with a man?"
Aunt: "Yes, it is, Angie."
Angie: "Well, it's not that I don't want to die and go to heaven with Jesus, but I do want to sleep with a man first."

■ DISCOVER AND "UNLEARNING"

An interesting book was written a generation ago entitled, *What We Learn from Children*. Rasey and Menge, the authors, emphasized the discovery method of learning:

Finally we have had to revise our thinking about the role of the teacher or nurturer. The learner does the learning. Teachers do not teach him. He is his own teacher.[2]

The discovery method of learning works better when we don't have to unlearn. But sometimes unlearning is a necessary skill. I grew up, for example, with such statements as, "Everything that goes up must come down," and, "He doesn't even know which way is up!" The space age has required me to "unlearn" the assumptions on which those statements were made. Rasey and Menge quote Jose Ortega y Gasset on this subject:

The man who discovers a new scientific truth has previously had to smash almost everything he had learned, and arrives at the new truth with hands blood-stained from the slaughter of a thousand platitudes.[3]

Perhaps children can discover truth better because they do not have as many platitudes to slaughter as adults do. Children arrive fresh as learners.

The followers of the Pharisees in first-century Palestine "knew" that legalism was the right way to live. They had *learned* that. The followers of the Sadducees "knew" there was no such thing as the resurrection. Even the disciples of Jesus "knew" he was too busy to be bothered with the presence of little children. We may have learned many fallacies by the time we get to be adults.

The fact that children come fresh to a situation lets

them see it as it is. A college student reported how a child helped her to see the truth more clearly:

I was baby-sitting in my home and my mom and I were talking about how I wanted to tell a certain guy that I really didn't want to go out with him. The guy called one day and my mother answered the phone, and I told Mom to tell him I wasn't home. The little boy I was baby-sitting for came up to me—I guess he had been listening to our conversation, because he said, "You know, Paula, you can't tell him you don't want to go out with him if you don't talk to him." It made me stop to think how much truth came from that statement.

Now, Paula probably knew that truth. But it was not fresh and clear to her prior to the child's intervention, because it lay hidden on her landscape which was cluttered with other learnings—perhaps ones like these: "I need to avoid touchy situations," or "It is a good idea to put off telling someone what he needs to know if it might hurt his feelings."

■ USING—NOT JUST STORING—INFORMATION
Caroline Pratt's book, *I Learn from Children*, was written about her experiences in starting a private school in New York City:

But the mere accumulation of information was not our purpose. We were not training for a Quiz Kids program—or its equivalent of that time or any time, the outpouring of streams of unrelated facts for the entertainment of adults. I have always been deeply sorry for the "bright" child. Most precocity is the fault of misguided adults; an encounter with one of these painfully swollen little egos can give no pleasure to one who has any respect for children.

But to know something and to be able to relate and use that knowledge is the beginning of learning to think.[4]

This same truth was stated in a different way by William Kingdom Clifford in 1868 in a Royal Institution lecture. He pointed out that the

. . .first condition of mental development is that the mind should be creative rather than acquisitive, that intellectual food should go to form mental muscle, rather than mental fat.[5]

Children, when left to their own curiosity, are more interested in building mental muscle than in storing mental fat. They are especially opposed to displaying such storage. Many parents try, unsuccessfully at times, to get their children to demonstrate their knowledge to others. Some children do not even want to "show" their learning to their own parents:

As a new mother, I took my cues from other mothers as to what I might work on with my son. So at the time they were learning numbers and ABCs, I kept doing little activities with my son, and he kept ignoring me; so I decided he just wasn't developmentally ready. I was surprised when one day I was in an adjoining room and heard him counting 1, 2, 3, etc. I later saw him pointing to the letters in his books saying A, etc., correctly. But when I went into the room he quit saying them. He knew them; he just wasn't ready to share his knowledge with me yet.

There is something to be said for this child's (and other children's) humility. It seems inappropriate to show off what one knows.

Being able to *use* information, however, can be extremely valuable, as this adult remembers from his childhood:

My dad and I were checking snares. I was five years old at the time and went to kindergarten in the mornings. As I remembered this particular occasion, we left home about 2:30 in the afternoon. It was in the dead of winter in northern Minnesota.

We lived on the edge of town and had to walk approximately a half mile or so to an abandoned streetcar line or roadbed. Of course, there was a lot of snow. Shortly after walking along this roadbed, we headed into a wooded area on what was to be a circular route. Dad knew where he had placed the snares on these various runways.

A little while later we came across some footprints in the snow. Dad realized these tracks were ours from just a short time before. To my amazement, he said we were lost and it would take a long time to get back, because we had to retrace our steps and it would be dark before we got home.

Conclusion—I shinnied up a tree and saw the telephone poles along the road and was able to direct our way back.

■ ASKING QUESTIONS

An accurate indicator of depth of thinking is the quality of questions one asks. One parent says he does not ask his children, "What's one thing you learned in school today?" but rather, "What's one question you asked in school today?"

Two-year-olds can ask questions that adults have great difficulty answering, e.g., "Why is Captain Hook [in *Peter Pan*] so mean?" This is a theological question dealing with the presence of evil in the universe. It isn't just that we need to couch the reply in words a two-year-old can understand—admittedly, that makes it harder—but it is, *in itself*, a difficult question.

Children can teach us a great deal with their "why" questions in terms of gathering information about cause and effect. They also can teach us to use "how" and "what" questions to help others gain insight into human behavior, their own and others.

There is a beautiful example of this given in a taped speech by Dr. Victor Cottrell, President of Ventures for Excellence, Lincoln, Nebraska. Vic was telling about a conversation he had years ago with his six-year-old daughter Cindy (now a college student). This conversation was about a patch of concrete by their house that adults call a driveway.

Note the excellent "what" and "how" questions Vic asks Cindy. He doesn't just tell her his point of view and his feelings. Rather, by his questions he helps her discover these things. Vic is a superb teacher. But the real stunner comes when Cindy responds in an entirely different way than Vic thought she would:

Cindy would never get her toys off the driveway. So I drove up one night after asking her many, many times, "Please get your toys out of the driveway." Sure as the world, there was the bicycle on the drive again. I drove up as close as I possibly could to it, but I didn't want to run over it because I knew she wouldn't be the one who would do the repairing. I had been teaching a class in communications that day in the college, and I decided I was going to try to practice what I had been teaching. I was really proud of myself.

I walked in and visited with my wife for a little bit and visited with Cindy. I picked her up in my arms and gave her a nice big hug and asked her how her day was. We had a nice time, and after about five or ten minutes I said, "Honey, how would it be if we went for a little walk together?"

She said, "Fine." Of course, I knew where we were going to walk. We walked out the front door and over into the driveway, and then she stopped and looked.

I said, "Honey, what do you see?" You know, the good old strategy of trying to get them to describe.

She said, "Well, I see my bicycle is in the driveway."

"*Yes, and my car is there too, isn't it? What could have happened to that bicycle?*"

"*Oh, you could have run over it.*"

"*Now how does Daddy feel about that?*"

"*Daddy doesn't like that at all.*"

"*Well, how do you feel about it?*" I was trying to get that ownership; now we're just about ready for the close—really bright guy.

She looked up to me with her little eyes and she asked, "*Dad, how much do you use this driveway?*"

Well, I thought, "*You know, I bet I use that 15 seconds in the morning, and maybe 15 seconds at night.*" And I said, "*Well. . . .*" I kind of stuttered around a little bit.

Then she used a follow-through question, "*Dad, do you know how much I use this driveway, and how much my friends use this driveway?*"

I kind of stuttered again.

"*We use this all day. That's one of the things you are trying to teach me. You don't like us playing out in the road.*"

"*No, I don't like you playing out in the road.*"

"*Well, this is our best place to play.*"

Suddenly, it finally hit me, "*I don't have a driveway, I have a* playway! *And, if I'm really on my very best behavior, I may be able to convince my child to allow me to move through her playway once in awhile!*"

When we see the world through the eyes of a child and we really listen and we really strive to understand, they may see that world about ten times clearer than we ever saw it. Why should we as adults have this funny idea that we ought to call that thing by the side of the house a driveway? That is adult mentality; it's really not describing its use. From that day on, I started thinking about our driveway as our playway and that made a tremendous difference in my attitude. It made a great difference in the way I saw those toys on the driveway, and quite frankly, I did not become frustrated anymore. Communication changes us. . .but we need to understand the world *that the other person is in, and we need to be open to change our way of looking at the world.*[6]

Cindy, of course, used the same method of asking questions that her father used, to help him discover a whole new way of looking at his world.

Fortunately, Vic listened carefully. Not all adults do that. Some of us may be like the following mother:

My son, at age six, talked about his new pet, Harvey. Being busy, I only half-listened until putting his clean underwear away one day. There was a black snake with yellow eyes looking at me! I screeched and threw clothes everywhere. He sauntered in and said with his six-year-old wisdom, "I told you I was keeping Harvey in my dresser drawer and you said it was OK." That certainly taught me to listen more carefully before saying, "Uh huh." It also took some explaining that Harvey would die in the drawer and needed to be outside with his relatives. My son saw the light, and transferred him to a basket on the porch. By morning Harvey was gone and a frantic search revealed nothing. He missed him for several days and then forgot about him. I never did! Six more gray hairs. Listening accurately may be the first step to knowledge and wisdom.

BECOMING CHILDLIKE

WE ARE ALL OF THE RIVER *

ne of the children we can learn from is ourselves. We can get in better touch with the child that we were during our growing-up days; but the process is not without some risk.

There may be some who feel they have cut themselves off from their growing-up families, or that they have been cut off. For example, you may feel there is no potential reconciliation with one or more people in your growing-up family and you may not want to begin getting images of your own childhood. There is a risk here; it is possible to think back to your childhood and open a bigger wound than can be immediatly sutured. On the other hand, the wound may be open already, and simply need to be studied, cleaned, and healed. Only you can make the judgment as to whether the risk is worth it. There may be some painful memories coming out of your past. If so, it would be helpful to have a close family member, a friend, or a counselor with whom to talk over these memories.

Although the memories come flooding back for many, there are others who cannot remember their childhood well. A college student was unable to remember any

*I am indebted to Char Merideth Hartzell (*Faith At Work*, January/February 1981, p. 10) for this way of describing life.

memories before the age of ten; the early years were so painful that these memories had been repressed. She used some of the methods outlined below to uncover some of her memories.

■ GETTING IN TOUCH

There are a number of methods of getting in touch with the child we once were and thereby learning from that child. Among these are the following:

1. Look over your old pictures. These pictures may be from your baby book, family albums, school pictures, year books, old newspaper clippings, and from many other sources. Ask someone—a family member or close friend—to sit down with you and look at these. That person may pick up information from the pictures that you do not see.

As you look at your old baby pictures, study your face. What kinds of emotions, if any, do you see? Can you let yourself feel friendly toward that infant? This is not easy; often infants are treated more like pets than equals. There is even a considerable prejudice against infants that shows up in the word "infantile." George Groddeck wrote fifty years ago about this prejudice:

If we allowed ourselves to realize once a day what a child is able to achieve we might gradually acquire some insights into the nature of children, gradually come to rejoice in what is fresh and childlike in our own natures, and even invent some better word in place of. . .infantile. . . .We are all infantile, thank God! We could not even continue to exist, much less accomplish anything, were it not so. The essential life of any man depends upon the degree to which he has been able to remain childlike, infantile, in spite of the blunting influences of adult life.[1]

As you look at pictures of you as a child with your family, from the family albums and perhaps from old suitcases, what do you see about relationships? Are you typically standing next to the same person in your family? Who is touching and being touched? What do you think it felt like to be next to the person by whom you are sitting or standing? Look at the different heights of the people in the picture.

As you go over your school pictures from each year or from as many years as they were taken, line them up from youngest to oldest. What kind of "movie" do you see? At what ages were you fully able to express yourself? At what ages, if any, were you inhibited and faking it? Are there any of these pictures that you don't like? Is there any age at which you do not accept yourself? Now this is a crucial question because we are "all of the river." The person that I was in the third grade is as important to me now as the person I am *today* will be to me *tomorrow*. I do not accept myself fully until I accept myself at all ages, including the vision of myself at an advanced age.

This truth, that all of me is of the river, came home to me very strongly when I realized in my early thirties that I did not accept myself as I had been in eighth grade. I looked at that old black-and-white school picture of me at thirteen years of age. I was stooped over and wearing bib overalls when they were not cool. And it suddenly came to me that I didn't like that kid. I was embarrassed and ashamed. I remembered that my parents had taken me to a physician because they thought I had back trouble. But the ailment I was facing was not a physical one. Since I did not like myself at the time, I tried to appear smaller by stooping over; or maybe my bent-over position was symbolic of the inhibited, rigid, unreleased feelings I was having about myself at that time.

When I looked at that picture and had those feelings flood back through my memory in my early thirties, I sought healing. As I thought of myself in my thirties alongside myself at thirteen, I was able, through the grace of God, to reach out in my mind, hug that bent-over boy, and say to him, "I love you, Paul. Even though you are a scared kid and you don't like yourself, yet I love you." And at that point there was healing that came into my life and I was in touch with myself in a good way. The river was not choked at that point.

Then an interesting thing happened to me that I did not make sense of until many years later. I had been teaching in high schools for a number of years. I remember saying that I never wanted to work in a junior high school. Sometime after this experience of coming to terms with myself as an eighth grader, I went to my superintendent of schools and asked for a transfer to one of the junior high schools in the district. The insight that came to me later was that I could not work with persons who were at *the same age* that I was unable to accept in my own history. Once I was able to accept myself, and value myself as an eight-grader, I was able to work comfortably with junior high students.

2. Another method of learning from your past is to allow yourself to uncover old images of incidents that occurred in the past. If you do this after you have examined actual pictures, you will find that these images will occur more easily. One of my images is as a child, perhaps in the second grade. I was walking to school and found a bird that was hurt. I remember taking it to school and getting some help from the teacher and older children in nurturing that bird back to health. That memory is an important one to me because it says that I did care as a child, and that I reached out to helpless, hurting creatures.

One of the fun images of my childhood is from elementary school, about the time World War II was breaking out. I remember that a number of us in that one-room country school were very interested in bombing and what it would be like to be a bombardier. Several of us boys would climb up into a locust tree in the school yard and eat there from our lunch buckets. We had nearly a full hour for lunch. We would sit high up in that tree, where various branches met the trunk, talking about the world and thinking about important things. We also practiced being bombardiers. We did this by spitting at bugs on the ground, and the boy who would get the hit or the near hit gained considerable prestige. Perhaps it is the paradox of the memory that stays with me; we were engaged in imitating a warlike behavior; yet the setting was a very peaceful one.

Many people find it easier to bring up old images and stories of their childhood if they have someone with whom to talk. Others find it easier to do this by writing in a journal. Often this will depend on whether your strong learning channel is auditory or visual. At any rate, use whatever method works for you and see how many stories and images you can uncover of important times you had as a child, both the good times and the bad times. After you have allowed these stories to surface, look for common themes. Were there common emotions present in different stories? Did the incidents take place inside or outside? Were you often with the same family members or the same friends? What can you learn about life and about *you* from these stories? How are you different after these stories have surfaced than you were before? If healing was needed, have you allowed that to happen?

3. Another method of recovering your past is to do some memory work regarding the stories that were told you, and the books that were read to you or that you read. I have an old Bible story book that has been used so much, the binding is completely gone and the loose pages—torn, dog-eared, wrinkled—are bound together with a black satin ribbon. This is the Bible story book from which my father read to me when I was a child. I

would crawl up on his knees and ask him to read. The memories of those times are very strong. I remember that the Bible stories were sometimes scary, and at other times were very reassuring. I remember gaining a concept of who Jesus was and learning to respect and like him. I remember the touch of my father and the kindness with which he read. That memory is an important one for me. Who read to you? In the stories that were read to you, who were some of the main characters? Do the books that you remember help you to image interpersonal situations at that time in your life?

4. Another way to learn from the child you were is to correspond with your parents, if they are still living, or with older siblings or relatives in your extended family. One person in the Learning from Children class wrote after the class:

I am reevaluating my own concepts of my childhood by corresponding with my mother. I have talked with her some over the phone, but we are going to work together on some memories.

There is usually something quite healing about studying one's growing-up family. We observe strengths that we never knew were there. Those who have developed psychodrama say that we cannot understand an experience until we have lived through it twice. Studying the strengths of our family is a way to relive the experience we had with our family of origin.

These are just some of the methods available to you for getting in touch with the child you were and learning from that child. That child has a great deal to teach you as you find more and more ways to get back to the headwaters of the river that is your life.

ADULTS—
TEACHABLE AND UNTEACHABLE

ot all adults are teachable. One eight-year-old said, "I've tried to teach my mom and dad to turn off the bathroom light, but they still leave it on." How can we make the transition as adults from being unteachable to becoming teachable? One of the first steps in this transition seems to be a heightened awareness:

I'm trying to put into practice something my eighteen-month-old daughter has taught me many times, but I only became aware of it after class one evening. As I arrived home she met me at the door full of joy—smiling, laughing, and running with arms open wide. She made me feel so important. I'm going to practice making every person that walks through my doors feel important, especially my family as they arrive home from work or school.

This mother learned a great deal from her one-and-a-half-year-old daughter. Her insight that could change the quality of family life has to do with immediate recognition, welcome, and expressed warmth at times of family *regathering*. The first thirty seconds of the regathering time after school and work can determine the emotional atmosphere for the rest of the day. "She made me feel *so* important!" It was this feeling, brought about by an eighteen-month-old child, that released learning in the adult—*and* a plan of action.

■ THE TEACHABLE MOMENT

The adult's statement as to how she learned is absolutely fascinating—". . .something my. . .daughter has taught me many times, but I only became aware of it after class one evening." Her little girl had welcomed her with the same open arms many times. Why had not this teaching had its effect earlier? And, most important, why did it occur when it did?

This parent had been attending the Learning from Children class. We had talked in class about learning from children how to express love. Somehow it all came together for this mother that particular evening. She "saw" the same event occur again, and this time it held new meaning for her because *the teachable moment had arrived.*

Perhaps something happened such as happens when we begin to learn to read. We see these marks:

ol

and we think "a circle and a line." But later, as we learn to attach a symbolic significance to such marks, we mentally put them together in a different way:

d

and we read the letter "d"! What has changed? We "see" the same marks, but now we attach a *meaning* to those marks. *The teachable moment has arrived.*

■ BEING CHOSEN

In addition to heightened awareness and the teachable moment, another factor in the adult's readiness for learning seems to be the acceptance of an adult by a child. This choosing of the adult by a child opens the adult to be teachable, particularly in the area of giving priority to relationships over tasks. A hurried college student learned from a two-year-old the difference between the urgent and the important:

Being the busy college person that I am, I seldom find time to make it back home; but I have one incentive that draws me there more than anything else—my nephew. He is two years old, and is absolutely the neatest kid I've ever met. Each time I go home, I'm informed about all his unique baby acquisitions. This last weekend everyone was excited about his "rock-a-baby" phase, in which he enjoys being held and rocked.

On my way back to college at the end of the weekend, I jetted over to see my sister, left my car running, and ran inside. My nephew was just getting ready for bed. "Aunt Peg, rock-a-baby?" he inquired. It floored me to see this little guy asking explicitly for me. I put my stuff down and took him in my arms. A half hour later when my brother stopped by, I asked him to shut my car off. I wasn't in a hurry. Through this one little event, I discovered that the day is long enough for everything. Take time to rock the babies!

■ INVOLVEMENT

A book entitled *Kids Don't Learn from People They Don't Like* gives a great deal of statistical evidence to support that thesis. [1] Our collection of stories supports this point of view when applied to adult learners. An adult tends to be more teachable when she is with a child she likes and with whom she is involved. This friendly relationship usually results in the adult paying close attention to the teacher (child), maintaining visual contact and eye level, and being open to learn.

My cousin has a daughter named Anne who is very loving and also very bright. Because of her intelligence and energy, she can sometimes get under a person's skin when there are millions of things to do. One afternoon I was running about an hour late, and my sensitivity was worn off. Anne caught me coming in the door and wouldn't let me get anything done. After about twenty minutes I finally asked her to leave and not bother me anymore. I felt terrible after a while, but she came back in a few minutes and poked her head in the door and said, "We still love each other, don't we Greg?" I call that unconditional love. I learned to get a grasp on life when the world had me running and worn down, and to sit down and ask the Lord to take over. Anne is a precious little girl with a lot to teach me.

■ CHILDREN USUALLY DON'T TRY TO TEACH
One time when Robert Frost was teaching school, he sent one of his students to the library to get Mark Twain's "The Jumping Frog of Calaveras County." He then used that short story as a parable on teaching. He said the problem with many teachers was that they filled their students so full of buckshot that the pupils were deprived of their jump. Frost favored "tickling" his students. [2]

Children rarely stuff adults with facts. However, they manage to tickle adults in many different ways. This tickling sometimes brings about a transformation with a previously unteachable adult:

My grades were low, all my assignments were due, my job was boring, and I never thought of anyone else. As luck would have it, I was asked to spend an afternoon with a three-year-old.

"Oh, great!" I thought. I decided to take her to the park. She could entertain herself, right?

Upon our arrival, however, she helped me explore the grass, study the simple lines on the sidewalk, and enjoy the beautiful flowers in the garden. These simple things held such unique qualities that they added a new zest to my life. The huge problems didn't seem so demanding or depressing. To think that I learned this from a little child. Isn't that a wonderful thought?

Yes, that is a wonderful thought!

■ RESPECT FOR THE TEACHER

Our stories give hope that most adults can become teachable. One attitude more than any other can guarantee that each of us will indeed learn from children. That is an attitude of respect for children. If we look straight across at them, and at times even up to them, we will be in a learning position. Once we begin to view childlikeness as Jesus did—as a prerequisite for the kingdom of heaven—we will treat children with great respect.

THE GENTLE LIFE STYLE OF JESUS

*T*s there a place for a gentle spirit in a violent world?

Over the past twenty-five years I've talked with many families, most of them Christians. When I asked each person where the hurting was for him or her, many have reported violent acts, both verbal and physical, including the following:

Twelve-year-old to father: "It hurts me when you call me dumb or stupid."

Thirteen-year-old to older teenage brother: "It hurts me when you tease me so much."

■ THE ABSENCE OF VIOLENCE

Gentleness is first the absence of verbal and physical violence. Verbal violence can include teasing, if the teasing is fun only for the person doing it and not for the person being teased. Name-calling is another form of verbal violence. The old saying, "Sticks and stones may break my bones, but words will never hurt me," is, of course, untrue. Yelling is another form of verbal violence. Sarcasm is still another. Many people still suffer from sarcastic remarks made twenty years earlier.

The different forms of physical violence are well known. In either physical or verbal violence both the abused and the abuser are diminished as human beings.

■ A WAY OF BEING
But gentleness is more than just the absence of violence. Gentleness means being with people in a way that respects them and nourishes them. The last few years, because of witnessing an increasing amount of violence in families, I've been trying to learn more about gentleness. I've found that even a meaningful definition of the word is difficult to find. So I've begun to look at the life style of Jesus to learn what a gentle spirit does. Perhaps, like love, gentleness is best explained by a model:

Come to me, all of you who are tired from carrying heavy loads, and I will give you rest. Take my yoke and put it on you, and learn from me, because I am gentle and humble in spirit; and you will find rest. For the yoke I will give you is easy, and the load I will put on you is light (Matthew 11:28-30, TEV*).*

■ DEVELOPING A GENTLE LIFE STYLE
Kent Estes, who has been my colleague in this study on learning from children, and another close friend, and I have met regularly as a support group for five years. For two of those years we studied the life of Christ as set forth in the Gospels, and we considered the implications of that life for our own lives. As we studied together, I learned from the gentle life style of Jesus. And I noted that "gentle" is a word Jesus himself used (in the Matthew 11 passage quoted above) to describe the way he lived.

In addition to studying the life of Christ, I began to

examine my own roots. My father was a non-macho, gentle man. He did not seem to have a need to *prove* that he was a man. He knew that. So he was able to express tenderness and love.

So I have two models of a gentle life style—my father and Jesus. The latter is available to anyone willing to do an intensive Bible study on the life of Christ. Now, concerning a second model, let's suppose your same sex parent—your role model—was *not* a gentle person, was perhaps even violent. Then it may be useful for you to study other relatives or friends. This will allow you to pattern intentionally after gentle persons, as you seek to develop a gentle life style.

■ GENTLENESS IS...

Gentleness is being as concerned with kindness as we are with honesty. In a beautiful little book about reconciliation, *Treat Me Easy*, Earnest Larsen says:

It is impossible to be too honest; but it is very possible to be honest without being kind. . . . I'm sorry; I've got to call a spade a spade is the creed of some so-called honest people. But more often than not this means "In the name of honesty I will punish you." [1]

Gentleness is adopting the point of view, "Catch them being good." We all know the feeling of being caught when we've been doing something bad. But how many of us remember being caught when we were doing something good? It is one of life's serendipities to be caught in such circumstances. "Hey, you're doing a good job on that!" or, "I want you to know I'm really proud of you," builds strength in those we love.

Gentleness is that quality which comes from real strength, whereas harshness comes from macho (phony) strength. Jesus chose a strong, gentle life style rather than a weak, macho life style. Gentleness is a quiet confidence that keeps us from yelling or hitting. It is letting others know when we hurt. It is finding the courage to comfort and protect another person, even at some cost to ourselves. The beautiful example of a courageous, gentle two-year-old can lead the way:

One time my two-year-old daughter and I were sitting on our porch when the little neighbor girl, who is six, was walking down the sidewalk to visit us. Just at that moment a little white poodle came tearing around the side of the house and apparently was startled by the little girl, and immediately began barking loudly and frantically. I could see this really frightened the six-year-old and she came running and leaping up to our porch. I am somewhat ashamed to say I had the urge to laugh because it was such a little dog.

But my little girl jumped up and yelled, "No!" at the dog, and put her arms around the bigger girl and patted her back. The truly amazing aspect of this is that my daughter also is afraid of dogs. From this I learned how important and just plain nice it is to be considerate of another's feelings. I also learned that a two-year-old can exhibit altruistic behaviors by putting her own fears secondary to saving another the pain of fear. I felt that my two-year-old exhibited a higher morality than I felt inside of myself, and I decided that if ever again I saw a child afraid, even if it did not seem justified to me, I would comfort, not laugh.

Gentleness is not excusing a "short temper" as something that can't be helped. Henry Drummond in his classic commentary on 1 Corinthians 13, *The Greatest Thing in the World,* has some helpful reminders:

No form of vice, not worldliness, not greed of gold, not drunkenness itself, does more to un-Christianize society than evil temper. For embittering life, for breaking up communities, for destroying the most sacred relationships, for devastating homes, for withering up men and women, for taking the bloom off childhood, in short, for sheer gratuitous misery-producing power, this influence stands alone.[2]

It is, of course, possible to be angry and not know it, as the following story from *The Pace of a Hen*, by Josephine Moffett Benton, points out:

One little boy had called his mother back a half dozen times for another drink or another confidence, or to remind her she had forgotten to repeat, "The dark is kind and cozy." She was getting a little worn. Then he said, "Why are you mad, Mother?" She had been so sure that she was behaving in a calm and patient manner. "Why, what makes you think I am cross?" "You walk mad."[3]

As Henry Drummond points out in the same commentary mentioned above, we must go deeper than our anger:

Hence it is not enough to deal with the Temper. We must go to the source, and change the inmost nature. . . . Souls are made sweet not by taking the acid fluids out but by putting something in—a great Love, a new Spirit, the Spirit of Christ. Christ, the Spirit of Christ, interpenetrating ours, sweetens, purifies, transforms all.[4]

Gentleness is being thoughtful of the dignity and integrity of another person. A third-grade teacher told the following story about one such gentle child:

My student teacher is pregnant and the students in my class just started seeing the change in her body. One day we got into a discussion about babies. It was fascinating for me to watch

my students' expressions as they asked her questions about un-
born babies, for example: "How can babies grow when you
can't see them to feed them?" "How can babies move and kick
when they're not born yet?" My student teacher said she had
never realized before how innocent and open children are, and
how inquisitive and eager to learn they are.

At the end of their discussion, one little boy apologized to
me for not including me in the discussion, but since I wasn't
pregnant he was afraid he would ask me a question I couldn't
answer and would embarrass me in front of the whole class!

■ A HOPE I HAVE

Like many, many others, I am concerned about child
abuse. The suffering of the children of the world from
violence is indescribable. It is my hope that this book,
along with efforts by others, can make a difference in
the way *adults view children.* Many adults who abuse children do not abuse other adults. They evidently see children as being of less worth than adults. My hope is that
we can get more and more adults to view children as
equals, or better yet, as master teachers. Note some of
the end-of-course "I Learneds" from a member of the
Learning from Children class:

An important insight into full-time mothering: It's not all
"give." I can learn from the kids as well as teach them.

I learned to look at all children as having the potential to
teach me something; this raises my opinion of kids.

I learned to listen to and try to understand my little boy as
a real person, not in an indulging way.

These three things are basically the same (placing more value
on children as people), but they are specific ways I have changed
my thinking and actions as a result of the one major insight.

The person who wrote this "I Learned" is gentle. Yet, by coming to view all children as teachers, she was able to raise her opinion of them.

An abusive adult has to "look down" to do violence to a child. Let's team up to help more and more adults look up to children as teachers. By following Jesus' command to become like little children, by encouraging others to do so, and by modeling a gentle life style, perhaps we can reduce the incidence of violence toward children.

May you always be joyful in your union with the Lord. I say it again: rejoice! Show a gentle attitude toward everyone. The Lord is coming soon (Philippians 4:4, 5, TEV).

THE CHILDLIKE ADULT

uriosity! I love to go through the aisles in a toy store. And I love to go to the library. I'm curious about what's in each one of those books, and I'm frustrated that I can't read them all, and that I can't do it right now. And tears—I finally learned to cry again. Somewhere I got the idea that adults weren't supposed to cry and I didn't, and things dried up inside. My father died when I was twenty-one and I cried, and I thought I had gone through the grieving process. About six years later it hit me full force again and I cried, and I cried, and I cried. And I'm glad to say that I can cry. It feels good. It really does.

This is a childlike adult for whom the rhythm of healing and growth has become a way of life. How did she achieve this? And how may we become childlike? Another adult says a workable method is to keep the childlike traits we have, and seek to add others:

I have realized that I have childlike qualities that should be kept—even if people call them childish, and try to make me feel ashamed of not "acting my age." There are also qualities that I should change. Not showing affection, and my inability to cry are two emotions I am working on. I have learned much more about myself and am not afraid to face the past. Being with children has given me an insight into young feelings and emotions.

■ THE PRESENT MOMENT

Infants and very young children are here and now persons. They think in one tense (the present) rather than three (past, present, and future). What would it be like to be *bound* in our thinking to the here and now? Well, it would have some obvious disadvantages, such as causing us to run up our credit card charges, since we would be unable to visualize consequences. But it would be a boost toward childlikeness.

I believe in miracles. Many miracles are repeatable, but the miracle of the present moment is not. We have one chance at that moment. So for the last several years I have had this motto sitting on my desk in a 5″ x 7″ frame, as a reminder:

THE PRESENT MOMENT
IS AN
UNREPEATABLE MIRACLE

A basis for this motto is Psalm 118:24, "This is the day the Lord has made; let us rejoice and be glad in it" (NIV). A day, or a moment, is the gift of life from God. As adults we sometimes have to relearn how to have a good time in the present moment:

When I asked my husband what he had recently learned from one of our children, he said he had learned how to have a good time. Our six-year-old son has a good time no matter what he's doing. He collects worms as Dad digs potatoes, and he collects and names caterpillars. Our son's excitement about our world has taught Dad to relax.

Another adult spoke in a similar way about learning to have a good time:

I'm realizing that I need to reorganize my time and reset my priorities. I won't say I don't have any fun in my life because I have—but I have always felt that I should get my work done first and then play. Well—now I am sure my work will still be there for me when I get back from "smelling the flowers"! It will get done eventually.

■ SPECIFIC SUGGESTIONS FOR BECOMING CHILDLIKE

In our Learning from Children class we asked the participants to brainstorm ways to release childlike characteristics. Here are some of the ideas they generated. Look them over and see if any of the suggestions captivate you.

Find the courage to take risks.

Make a choice whether you want to be childlike or not.

Keep contact with children. Grandparents whose own children are gone, or singles, or couples without children can take advantage of relating to children by teaching a church school class.

Have very close friends with whom you can really relax, and with whom you don't have to dress up; in these situations it is easy to be creative and silly.

Teach your own childhood to your children as a heritage and enjoy the process; for instance, teach them the games you played as a child. Another way to do this is to teach the last generation's holiday traditions to younger children.

Join a creative group such as an arts council to help you release your creativity.

Take the risk to do childlike things, such as taking piano for eight years, after years of fear. By taking risks the first time, confidence is built up to continue.

Sing, dance, and yell.

Love and give love by touching, hugging and kissing.

Use playfulness, cheerful movement, silliness.

Keep senses alert to stimuli.

Active people tend to be more childlike. They are creative because they are into constant movement and "doing" things.

Follow the examples of a child or childlike adult. When you see a childlike quality exhibited by another, feel free to model it.

Childlikeness can be released when certain conditions are met, for example, when inhibiting adults are not present. Feeling relaxed and safe helps.

Read children's literature for your own enjoyment—let the child within you enjoy it.

When the lights are out and visual distractions are eliminated (no one sees what we look like) it is easy to laugh and cut up.

We can work best at the process when:

- *we are with our children, or our brothers and sisters*
- *we are around other childlike people and they inspire and influence us*
- *we are with friends and there is a camaraderie*
- *we are being creative*
- *we are happy with ourselves and not under a lot of stress*
- *we gain awareness that releases these traits*

There are some recurring themes among these suggestions. One is risk. Becoming childlike is a risky business. Another theme has to do with maintaining contact with children or with our own family members, including the family we grew up in. Other themes include becoming more active, and choosing to be with people who release rather than inhibit us.

Certain readers may find "Ideas for Further Action and

Study"in Appendix One useful in the process. Those suggestions are not for everyone. The systematic, analytical person
will probably find them more helpful than the random, intuitive learner.

■ THE CONTINUING PROCESS

Two years ago I began to take seriously Jesus' statement
that it was necessary to become like a little child to enter
the kingdom of heaven. That decision has made some
differences in my life:

1. I'm exchanging my sedentary life style for a more
active one. This has included becoming a part of a group
exercise program.

2. I am expanding my point of view that children are
learners, to include the concept that they are also teachers. Now when I enter the presence of a child, I am
aware that the possibility is there for me to learn, find
healing, and grow.

3. We are working in our church to expand our view
of Christian education to include the idea that following
Christ requires adults to learn from children and to become childlike. One of our church boards now has among
its written goals:

*Each member of this board is encouraged to get down on eye
level with at least one child every Sunday morning.*

Two weeks ago when I did this, a three-year-old girl
came up to me and hugged me. Her warmth and acceptance helped me realize again that I was lovable. Last
week a three-year-old boy who had just returned from
camping and fishing with his parents told me he had
caught a fish that "was bigger than me and my brother
and my mom and my dad!" His joy and excitement en-

ergized me. Amazing things begin to happen when we enter the world of a child. Both the child and the adult are enriched.

4. I am continuing to collect stories concerning what adults are learning from children. This process is useful to me, and it helps the adults who contribute the stories begin to view children as teachers.

5. I have begun the process of seeking out and studying adults who are childlike. This is a bit like getting one's first view of mountains. It is a magnificent, breathtaking scene. A long time will be needed to "take it all in." This will be the next part of my own journey into childlikeness.

If the quest looks attractive to you, I invite you to commit yourself to the venture. Simply begin at the place that appears the most exciting to you.

IDEAS FOR FURTHER
ACTION AND STUDY

Here are some ideas for continuing the process of becoming childlike. Children act first and then study (to
answer the questions raised by their actions). That se-
quence also works well for adults who want to become
like children.

■ ACTION

1. If you do not have weekly access to children, plan
to gain such access. Here are some ideas:
   a. Get down on eye level with at least two preschool
      children at morning worship each week. Work at
      getting some interaction going—touch, talking, or
      listening.
   b. Volunteer to be an assistant or teacher in a chil-
      dren's church school class.
   c. Sit on your front porch instead of your patio.
   d. Spend an hour or two a week as a volunteer at an
      elementary school or daycare center.
   e. Talk and play with the children at family reunions
      and other family gatherings.
   The important thing in spending time with children
is to do it not just as an observer but as a participant.
Instead of trying to learn something from them, try to

make your time with them a significant, worthwhile time for both of you. Open yourself to listening to them, to viewing them as master teachers, and the learning will happen.

2. When the learning does happen, begin to write your stories about what you learned from a child, and share them with at least one other adult.

3. Go over again the qualities that are mentioned in chapters 3-21 and select two or three you would like to work on. Then choose a child to be your mentor in each area. Make this choice based on your judgment of which child is an especially good pattern for you in expressing love, or arousing laughter, for example. Then spend time with that child and expect that you will grow in that particular quality.

4. Work within your church to help the Christian education committee to view children as an important resource in teaching adults. How many churches throughout the world are taking seriously Jesus' statement that we need to become like little children to enter the kingdom of heaven? You can help your church do this.

5. Benson and Stewart in their book, *The Ministry of the Child*, suggest a "Six-Session Course for Group Study" within a church setting to help adults utilize the ministry of children. This course has excellent potential for church groups.

■ STUDY

There are many childlike traits mentioned and discussed in chapters 3-21: humility, trust, honesty, optimism, courage, placing relationships over tasks, expressing love, caring, friendliness, sense of wonder, touch, laughter, sensitivity, forgiveness, mourning, ability to heal brokenness, moving, playing, singing, creativity, and the thirst for learning.

There are several ways you can study these childlike qualities either by yourself, or preferably in a group. This group can be made up of friends, work colleagues, church school class, or some other study group.

1. Using this book as a study source, begin with chapter 3 and discuss or reflect on the stories and ideas about humility. Begin to tell your own stories of your interaction with children and what you learned from them. This storytelling is a very important part of the learning process, both for the storyteller and for the other members of the group. Summarize on a chalkboard or newsprint the important learnings about humility.

Then using this same method, go to chapter 4 (on trust) at the next meeting of the group, and so on through the rest of the childlike qualities.

2. Do a Bible study of the life of Jesus from one of the Gospels. Note the childlike qualities you see in his life—his gentleness, honesty, caring, touch, etc. You can go through the Gospel of Mark in four months, studying one chapter a week.

3. Reread chapters 22-25, then begin a study of childlike adults. You probably already have a "feeling," an intuition, about who these childlike adults are. Another way to identify such persons is to work from the Contents page of this book. Anyone who has five to ten of the qualities noted there, and has them at a fairly deep level, would be useful to study. You may wish to use the Structured Interview guide in Appendix Two. Ask a childlike person to visit your study group for a time of sharing. At the end of that time, give that person a standing ovation. It will probably be the first time in his or her life to receive such affirmation for being childlike.

4. Ask somebody to interview you using the Structured Interview guide. Begin in this way to study your own childlike characteristics.

STRUCTURED INTERVIEW
FOR USE WITH PERSONS
IDENTIFIED AS CHILDLIKE

We are studying people whom we think have carried into adulthood some childlike characteristics or qualities. We view such characteristics in a very positive way. Such qualities help adults to be all they are meant to be. We have some questions we hope will be useful in learning more about adults who have these qualities. First, do you have any questions about what we are trying to learn?

(Interviewer—the pronouns in this interview may be changed, so that you can interview a friend or family member of a childlike person, and ask that friend/family member *about* the childlike adult.)

1. What are some of the childlike qualities you see yourself as having? (Interviewer—at this point show the interviewee the Contents page of this book for a look at some of the childlike qualities.)

2. What are some of the childlike things that you do?

3. Were you aware prior to this interview that these traits were childlike?

4. What are some specific reasons that you have been able to keep (or regain) the childlike qualities in your life?

5. Do you view your childlike characteristics as an asset in life or a liability?

6. Has there been a time when you did not have this viewpoint about your childlike characteristics?

7. What are some childlike qualities, if any, that you feel you have lost?

8. What position do you have in the family (only, oldest, middle, or youngest)?

9. Are your parents childlike people?

10. Do you recall childhood as a positive or a negative time in your life?

11. Are there other members of your family who are or were childlike? Did you have a role model for your childlike characteristics?

12. Are you sometimes put down or rejected for displaying these qualities? If so, how do you deal with this?

13. Do you feel these traits are inhibited in any other way by people around you?

14. Are you more apt to be childlike around children or adults?

15. Is there something that you have learned from a child? If so, tell the story of how this happened.

16. What quality(ies) do you most admire in others?

17. What do you do when you don't have to do anything?

18. What are some of your lifetime or long-term goals?

19. How do you handle stress?

20. That's the end of the structured part of this interview. Do you have other things you would like to say about childlike qualities?

· N O T E S ·

CHAPTER 1
1. Ashley Montagu, *Growing Young* (New York: McGraw-Hill, 1981), p. 154.
2. Bruce MacDougall, *Rejoice in the Lord* (Nashville: Abingdon, 1979).
3. Ashley Montagu, *Growing Young* (New York: McGraw-Hill, 1981), p. 6.
4. Dennis C. Benson and Stan J. Stewart, *The Ministry of the Child* (Nashville: Abingdon, 1978 and 1979).
5. Robert Coles, *Children of Crisis* (Boston: Little, Brown and Co., five volumes, 1967—1977).
6. Robert Coles, *Sojourners*, May 1982, p. 14.

CHAPTER 2
1. Sister Jose Hobday, "The Spiritual Power of Story Telling, Part I" (Kansas City, Mo.: The National Catholic Reporter Publishing Co., 1980). This is Cassette Tape 1 of a two-tape kit.

CHAPTER 3
1. Dag Hammarskjöld, *Markings* (New York: Knopf, 1964), p. 174.
2. Toby Talbot (Ed.), *The World of the Child* (Garden City, N.Y.: Anchor Books, 1967), a chapter (unnumbered) by George Groddeck, "Man's Part As Child," p. 61.
3. Lawrence LeShan, *How to Meditate* (Boston: G. K. Hall & Co., 1974), p. 1.
4. *Ibid.*, p. 2.
5. This reference, and those immediately preceding, are from *Today's English Version*, the *Good News Bible*.
6. Bruno Bettelheim, *The Uses of Enchantment* (New York: Vintage Books, 1977).

CHAPTER 4
1. Matthew 5:3-10, from the *New International Version* of the Bible.

CHAPTER 6
1. Ashley Montagu, *Growing Young* (New York: McGraw-Hill, 1981), p. 181.
2. Bruno Bettelheim, *The Uses of Enchantment* (New York: Vintage Books, 1977), p. 125.

CHAPTER 7
1. From Jason Epstein, " 'Good Bunnies Always Obey': Books for American Children," in *Only Connect: Readings on Children's Literature*, Sheila Egoff, G. T. Stubbs, and L. F. Ashley (Eds.) (Toronto: Oxford University Press, Second Edition, 1980), p. 74.
2. Robert D. Strom, *Growing Together: Parent and Child Development* (Belmont, Cal.: Wadsworth Pub. Co., 1978), pp. 88, 89.
3. No author noted, *There Is a Rainbow Behind Every Dark Cloud*, Copyright by the Center for Attitudinal Healing (Millbrae, Cal.: Celestial Arts, 1978). The quote is from the Foreword, p. 3, by Gerald Jampolsky, M.D., and Pat Taylor.

CHAPTER 8
1. Charles E. Hummel, *Tyranny of the Urgent* (Madison, Wis.: Intervarsity Christian Fellowship, 1967), p. 4.
2. *Ibid.*, p. 6.
3. C. S. Lewis, *Chronicles of Narnia* (New York: Macmillan Pub. Co., 1970).
4. Verna Birkey and Jeanette Turnquist, *Building Happy Memories and Family Traditions* (Old Tappan, N. J.: Fleming H. Revell Co., 1980).

CHAPTER 9
1. Jack Balswick, *I Want to Say I Love You* (Waco, Tex.: Word, Inc., 1978).

CHAPTER 10
1. Ashley Montagu, *Growing Young* (New York: McGraw-Hill, 1981), p. 186.

CHAPTER 12
1. Dennis C. Benson and Stan J. Stewart, *The Ministry of the Child* (Nashville: Abingdon, 1978 and 1979), p. 12.
2. Rachel L. Carson, *The Sense of Wonder* (New York: Harper & Row, 1956), p. 45.

CHAPTER 14
1. Norman Cousins, *Anatomy of an Illness* (New York: Bantam, 1981), p. 84.

2. *Ibid.*, pp. 82, 83.

CHAPTER 15
1. Antoine de Saint Exupéry, *The Little Prince* (New York: Harcourt Brace Jovanovich, 1943, 1971), p. 17.
2. *Ibid.*, p. 17.

CHAPTER 17
1. Ashley Montagu, *Growing Young* (New York: McGraw-Hill, 1981), p. 35.
2. Kent Estes, unpublished poem, "The Death of My Mother . . . The Birth of My Son," 1978.

CHAPTER 19
1. Dennis C. Benson and Stan J. Stewart, *The Ministry of the Child* (Nashville: Abingdon, 1978 and 1979), pp. 92, 93.
2. Jerome L. Singer, quoted in "Practical Applications of Research," newsletter of Phi Delta Kappa's Center on Evaluation, Development, and Research, Bloomington, Indiana, Vol. 5, No. 2, December 1982, p. 3.

CHAPTER 20
1. Betty Edwards, *Drawing on the Right Side of the Brain* (Boston: Houghton Mifflin Co., 1979).
2. Robert D. Strom, *Growing Together: Parent and Child Development* (Belmont, Cal.: Wadsworth Pub. Co., 1978), pp. 87, 88.
3. *Ibid.*, p. 88.

CHAPTER 21
1. From Norman Cousins, *Human Options* (New York: W. W. Norton & Co., 1981), p. 24.
2. Marie I. Rasey and J. W. Menge, *What We Learn from Children* (New York: Harper & Brothers, 1956), p. 39.
3. *Ibid.*, p. 40.
4. Caroline Pratt, *I Learn from Children* (New York: Cornerstone Library Publications, 1948, 1970), pp. 46, 47.
5. Quoted in Ashley Montagu, *Growing Young* (New York: McGraw-Hill Book Co., 1981), p. 78.
6. Dr. Victor Cottrell, "Qualities of Family Life," a cassette tape (Ventures for Excellence, Inc., 1620 So. 70th St., Lincoln, NB 68506).

CHAPTER 22
1. Toby Talbot (Ed.), *The World of the Child* (Garden City, N.Y.: Anchor Books, 1967), a chapter (unnumbered) by George Groddeck, "Man's Part As Child," p. 61.

CHAPTER 23
1. David N. Aspy and Flora N. Roebuck, *Kids Don't Learn from Teachers*

They Don't Like (Amherst, Mass.: Human Resource Development Press, 1977).

2. Nancy Vogel, *Robert Frost, Teacher* (Bloomington, Ind.: Phi Delta Kappa, 1974), p. 16.

CHAPTER 24

1. Earnest Larsen, *Treat Me Easy* (Liguori, Mo.: Liguori Publications, 1975), pp. 86, 87.
2. Henry Drummond, *The Greatest Thing in the World* (New York: The Greystone Press, 1951), pp. 50, 51.
3. Josephine Moffett Benton, *The Pace of a Hen* (Philadelphia: United Church Press, 1961), pp. 33, 34.
4. Henry Drummond, *The Greatest Thing in the World* (New York: The Greystone Press, 1951), pp. 56, 57.